WHY DO SMART

STUPIꓷ

PEOPLE MAKE SUCH

STUPIꓷ

MISTAKES?

A practical negotiation guide
to more profitable client relationships
for marketing and communication agencies,
sales teams and professional service people

Chris Merrington

D1412851

Cover design and book design by Neil Coe
Illustrations by Noel Ford

First published in 2011

Ecademy Press
48 St Vincent Drive, St Albans, Herts AL1 5SJ
info@ecademy-press.com
www.ecademy-press.com

Printed and bound by: Lightning Source in the UK and USA

Printed on acid-free paper from managed forests. This book is printed on demand, so no copies will be remaindered or pulped

ISBN 978-1-907722-01-1

Dedication

To my wonderful clients who have shared with me their negotiation and business stories and the mistakes they have made.

To those clients of mine who now negotiate more effectively and profitably.

To my bosses who tolerated my mistakes (well, those they knew about!) and let me learn from those mistakes.

To my friends and clients who helped in the writing and editing of this book.

Thank you.

Praise for this book

"This is great – more than a book on negotiation – it should be a bible for all agency account handlers. Inspiring and practical."
Tara Page, Client Services Director, Saatchi and Saatchi Health

"Moving from supplier to partner should be the goal of any forward-thinking agency – the thoughtful and practical advice here can really help to make that goal a reality."
Phil Bartlett, General Manager, Torre Lazur McCann
McCann World Group

"Chris Merrington knows his sector inside out and has great strategies, tools and approaches that actually solve the problems. And I know because I've tried them."
Martin Finn, Managing Director, EdComs

Chris Merrington

After 20 years in a successful agency career at director level in client management and business development, Chris started Spring 80:20 in 2001. Spring 80:20 Limited specialises in working with directors of communication agencies, sales teams and professional services enabling them to be more successful, more productive and more profitable.

Spring 80:20 has worked with over 60 agencies, large and small – both independents, regional agencies and network groups such as Omnicom, Engine, Interpublic and Publicis.

Chris works with all types of agencies:

- Advertising

- Media

- Direct marketing

- Digital

- Design

- Promotional marketing

- Research

- Sponsorship

- Field marketing

- Experiential

He has worked with agency trade bodies such as the IPA (Institute of Practitioners in Advertising) and the IPM (Institute of Promotional Marketing).

Chris has worked with agencies across Europe from Moscow to Germany, from Turkey to Spain.

Spring 80:20 has also worked with corporate clients such as The Telegraph, EMAP, Zurich Insurance, M&G and the Times Educational Supplement.

Spring 80:20 Limited

Spring 80:20 provides training for communication agencies, sales teams and professional services in key areas such as:

- Negotiation skills
- Trusted adviser selling
- Selling consulting services
- Winning new business
- Leading and managing a great team
- Passionate persuasive presentations
- Developing existing clients
- Dealing with difficult people
- Being effective under pressure

More importantly, much of Spring 80:20's business, over 90% in fact, comes from repeat business and referrals. Clients consistently talk about the difference Spring 80:20 has made to their business.

To learn more about Spring 80:20's work go to:

www.spring8020.co.uk or contact
Chris at: chris@spring8020.co.uk   Telephone +44 (0) 1932 880312

What clients say about Spring 80:20's training

"I am certain the course will help us make a real change to the business and deliver tangible results to the bottom line – we recovered the costs of the course within 24 hours."
Group Finance Director, Cogent Elliott, Integrated Advertising Agency

"Your experience of agency life was a real benefit and hit the spot with our senior team... people could immediately put what they had learnt into practice."
Director, Fishburn Hedges, Omnicom. PR Agency

"I can confidently say that the course has paid for itself several times over in the first few weeks."
Managing Director, Gyro:HSR, Integrated Agency

"The sales executives have put into action what they have learnt... In the first week after training we calculated a real increase in sales of over £40,000."
Learning & Development, Telegraph Media Group

Content

Preface

This book is written to help you:

- Make more money

- Make more profit

- Improve your relationships with your clients

- Deliver more value

- Have more confidence

- Increase your self-belief

Does that seem like an exaggeration or an over-claim? Do the techniques in this book really work, even in a recession? Yes, absolutely, and even more so in tough times!

They become especially crucial if you want a long-term, sustainable, profitable business.

How can I be so sure? For over 20 years I worked in agency client management and then business development at director level in several leading marketing communication/direct marketing agencies. I worked with clients in business-to-business, consumer marketing and also government departments – with companies ranging from Yellow Pages to Pizza Hut to the Central Office of Information. I made many mistakes, stupid mistakes looking back. In hindsight, many of these mistakes are now my best learnings.

I've consulted and trained literally thousands of people in agencies and sales people to negotiate more effectively.

The agencies have ranged from advertising to direct marketing, from design to public relations, from promotional marketing to sponsorship, from digital to research and experiential in the UK and across Europe.

The agencies consistently tell me afterwards, how much difference these negotiation skills have made to their business, their confidence, their client relationships and, of course, their agency's profitability.

Clients are buying better and negotiating more aggressively than ever before. They are more aware of their power and are using it to good effect. Agencies need to be better prepared than ever before to negotiate with these clients if they want to stay one step ahead of the game.

I've consulted many times with agencies on their dealings with their clients' Procurement departments. Often these purchasing specialists are formidable negotiators, putting their suppliers under considerable pressure.

Is this book only for agency people? No, I've consulted and trained the sales teams of major corporate companies including The Telegraph and EMAP, enabling their sales people to negotiate more effectively with their clients and customers. This book will be useful to anyone in professional services who advises and consults clients – business consultants, accountants, architects and lawyers.

I've even consulted with one company on their negotiations with a major union. To my delight, the strategies and techniques held true even in the negotiations with union officials.

One of my clients systematically tracked and measured the improvement in sales of their sales team, their ability to sell and negotiate better. Their people achieved an average increase in sales of over £40,000 in the first week after my workshops for every 10 participants on our consultative selling and negotiation workshops. This was at the start of the recession in summer 2008-2009 – a challenging time to sell and negotiate.

"I wish I'd known then what I know now" – if I had known what I know now when I worked in agencies selling to clients, I would have been even more successful, even more profitable, won even more business and received even bigger bonuses!

Will these techniques work all the time? No, probably not. But they will work the majority of the time, perhaps 80-85 % of the time. Those are pretty good odds, I reckon.

Will these techniques work outside of the work environment? The techniques and strategies are certainly transferable to other areas within your life. I've used some of the negotiation principles and techniques to good effect in the process of refurbishing a property and dealing with hotels and shops. Some of the techniques can even help you in negotiating with the toughest of all negotiators – your children. For example, your ability to know when and how to say 'no' to your children will have a huge impact on the quality of your lives as parents and their lives as individuals.

I wish you well in your negotiations. Let me know how you get on and send me your negotiation stories and experiences. All stories sent in will receive a Spring 80:20 small jar of honey. Send your negotiation story to Chris@spring8020.co.uk (I'll tell you all about the relevance of the honey later).

It's not what you know – it's what you do with what you know

My hope is that when you have read this book you are pleased by what you've learnt for your time and effort invested. However, if you do nothing with what you've learnt, if you don't turn your learnings into actions, then really it was just an academic exercise.

An analogy I often use in workshops is that anyone can join a gym, buy the trainers, the kit and iPod. That's the easy part and sadly it won't get you fitter. The hard part is going to the gym regularly two or three times a week.

Similarly I encourage you to:

First, decide what outcomes you want from reading this book.

Secondly, commit to yourself that you will act on at least three key learnings.

Thirdly, continue to develop your negotiation skills as a crucial life-skill.

CHAPTER 1

Why do smart people make such stupid mistakes?

Key points in this chapter

- Heightened awareness of the mistakes we can so easily make when negotiating with clients

- The opportunity to reflect on which of the mistakes are ones you are making and need to avoid

Let's look at the typical mistakes people, including smart people, make when selling and negotiating in the service industry and agencies especially. Then, in the other chapters of the book, we will consider how best to avoid and learn from these mistakes.

It's not dumb to make a mistake. If you never make mistakes you are probably not taking enough risks and aren't pushing yourself enough. However, what is really dumb is to repeat the same mistake over and over again. It's dumb not to learn from our mistakes. It's dumb not to observe, reflect, think and change your behaviour when you can see a particular action or strategy isn't working well. So why do we find it so hard to learn from our 'negotiation' mistakes?

I've worked with many really smart people within agencies and in sales teams of many leading companies. However, I see the same mistakes being made in most of those companies, often over and over again. These smart people are generally making quite good money from their clients; however, they could be making so much more. Much of this book is common sense, yet it often isn't common practice.

Here are the typical mistakes smart people make. In the rest of the book we will discover what the best practice techniques and strategies should be to avoid these mistakes.

Mistake 1: Price crumbling

How well do you hold your prices?

Clients and customers will challenge your price; it's part of their job to do so. However, price crumbling too quickly will cost you dearly. The more you drop your price and the quicker you drop your price, the more the client will expect you to drop your price even further. Clients will see your willingness to drop your price, not as generosity, but that your original price was over-inflated or had so much fat built in that you could easily afford to lose some of it.

Does this mean you should never drop your price? Of course not, there are specific strategies to apply if you do need to drop your price. Even dropping your price by as little as 1 % or 2 % can have a major impact on your overall bottom line profitability.

Imagine you are looking to buy a new house or flat. You go to see one priced at £300,000 which you like and decide to put in an offer. You decide to put in an aggressive offer of £250,000 expecting it to be refused. Instead the vendor enthusiastically says 'OK.' Instead of feeling delighted, you are now thinking you should have gone even lower and that maybe something is wrong with the property as the vendor seems so desperate to sell. The relationship and trust between buyer and seller is not looking good.

Yet how often do we do something similar for clients, agreeing to provide essentially the same proposal but matching their lower budget rather than our original proposed higher price?

During the recession, agencies told me their clients had threatened them that they had to reduce their fees by 20 %, 30 %, 40 % and even 50 %. If you are over-dependent on that client, you are left with little alternative but to comply.

Most people price crumble – often in the belief that they will lose the deal unless they drop their price. Whether it is from desperation or in order to show the client how keen we are to work with them, we often drop our price. The paradox is that the more we drop our price, the more the client wants us to drop our price still further. So will we lose a deal if we don't drop our price? Maybe, maybe not. Dropping our price too easily creates mistrust and can seriously damage the relationship rather than strengthen it. If you don't believe in the value you provide, then why should anyone else?

General Motors instructed all their agencies in the US in 2008 that their fees would be reduced by 20% due to poor sales in the automotive industry. How would you respond if your client demanded that of your agency? (A 20% drop in the revenue from this client will impact your profitability significantly more than 20%.) For many companies which make less than 20% profit this may mean losing money.

Is this the ultimate in price crumbling? (Self-imposed)

One agency was so desperate to win an important new high-profile client (having lost several major clients in a short period) they offered to charge no fees to this new client for the first year. At the end of the twelve months the plan was that the agency's fees would revert to their proposed normal level. Presumably they felt this would be a year-long opportunity to demonstrate how good the agency was and that the client would be so impressed they would hire them at the normal level of fee at the end of Year One. What do you think happened at the end of the year?

The client left and went to another agency.

When we give things away for free there is a danger that clients see the value as just that – free or zero.

When we come up against a tough negotiator who may use aggression, a tough negotiation stance and even threatening behaviour, it is so easy just to give in to their demands and drop our price. Subsequently, most of us regret that decision.

Decide in haste, repent at leisure.

Mistake 2: Lack of preparation

It is common to skip preparation before negotiation meetings and phone calls believing you can 'wing it' in the meeting – or worse still, on the phone.

Often it seems the more senior the person in the agency, or sales person, the more they think they can 'wing it.'

This can be exacerbated when two or more of you go to a negotiation meeting with clients and haven't prepared. You are likely to contradict each other.

There are few areas in life where preparation pays off more than in negotiations.

It will increase your confidence to negotiate, provide goals to aim for and help you anticipate possible actions, questions and challenges by the other party.

Mistake 3: Thinking great 'client service' is always saying 'yes'

What is the impact on your business of always doing your client's bidding and always giving them what they want?

When we join an agency in a junior role, typically we are told how important the big clients are and that 'whatever it takes' is the mantra.

Giving in 'for an easy life' is so common; however…

You get the behaviour you tolerate.

It is easy to make the mistake of doing what you think is right in the short term. However, you end up making life harder for yourself in the medium and long term.

Clients encourage this mistake. They want more for less. They seize every opportunity to squeeze more from each budget.

Sometimes, weak agency account management believes, incorrectly, that the way to retain clients is to do everything and anything clients want, even for an unprofitable fee. Great client management should really be about delivering value by the bucket-load at a fair price and a fair return for the agency.

Charge what you are worth not what you think they will pay.

Managing the expectations of your client is an important skill. Sometimes we over-promise through excitement, enthusiasm or naivety, or all three, and then either under-deliver – or worse, fail to deliver.

Giving in for an easy life has become a huge problem for agencies. Agencies are haemorrhaging profits by being too quick to say 'yes'.

Many account handlers are too passive and too reactive towards their clients. If you lack assertiveness in your negotiations, there is a high risk the other party will take advantage of your behaviour or, if nothing else, that you don't achieve the full potential of the deal for yourself.

Often this lack of assertiveness is combined with weak agency account management. We agree too readily to a client's demands from the fear of 'rocking the boat.' We don't charge for those 'minor changes' or the fourth set of amends. We don't question that unreasonable deadline or inadequate budget versus the client's requirements.

What happens when you give a child everything it wants, such as a new computer game, a new mobile phone, sweets, DVDs, fast food and always say 'yes' to their demands? In workshops when I ask this question I get the answer 'a monster' or 'a brat.'

Are there parallels with agency clients? By caving in and giving your client everything they demand, what might you turn your client into?

Excitedly, we win that new client after a gruelling pitch against tough opposition. We win that new client having impressed them with our strategic thinking, our insights into their business, our reputation, our creative ideas, our challenging perspective and our new-found business relationship.

We've developed and presented some of our best thinking and ideas. Our great fresh thinking impresses the client and they are convinced they are about to employ experts who really understand the client's business.

Then, perhaps two years later, there is a danger we become like a sausage machine. We simply implement and deliver 'sausages' – not the original reason we won the business in the first place.

We fall into the implementation trap.

We start to believe that our prime purpose is simply to implement. The sausage machine becomes increasingly efficient at producing sausages, which is fine while the client thinks they only want sausages. We continue to deliver what they want, not necessarily what they need.

When the client becomes bored of sausages or sausages are no longer required, they feel like they need a more varied diet and there is a risk they look elsewhere at other agencies.

Or it all seems fine until a new senior client decision-maker replaces our previous main contact and questions why they are employing expensive advisers to simply implement.

The acid test for an agency is when the senior client who appointed the agency leaves. How enthusiastically do the remaining members of the client team recommend your services to the new incoming senior client?

It is easy to be so busy delivering and implementing that we forget what it is that the client truly values. When your focus is simply to deliver and implement, this can impact your self-belief and confidence. Instead of knowing what your client needs, we make assumptions about those needs. This back-foot mindset weakens your ability and power to negotiate.

Do you know what your clients really value?

When did you last ask them?

What might happen if you said 'no'?

Mistake 4: Pressure can lead to wrong decisions

Many people working in agencies are under huge pressure from every angle.

That pressure can be to achieve specific financial targets in a world of increasing competition, pressure from clients to deliver and the desire to win new business at any cost.

The pressure can come from their boss, colleagues or simply from within themselves. Time pressure to deliver and tight deadlines exacerbate this situation.

When we are desperate for business or to make that sale, it is so easy to make wrong decisions and give the wrong impression to the other party. Under pressure we agree to deals which, long term, are unprofitable for us. Most of us find it so hard to walk away from a deal even if it means we will lose money if we agree to it.

No deal is better than a bad deal.

In the heat of a negotiation discussion about fees or rates, there can be a temptation to believe we must give immediate answers to every question we are asked and every demand made.

Our heart rate is racing, our blood pressure has increased and we can feel the perspiration on our forehead and the back of our neck. This all encourages us to give an instant snap decision. During this physiological reaction it is dangerous to make unplanned business decisions.

There is one thing worse that losing a new business pitch and that's winning an unprofitable new client.

Mistake 5: Not increasing fees and rates

I ask agencies, "When did you last increase the fee levels that you charge your clients?"

There are many agencies I meet who haven't increased their fees and rates to clients for four, five, even six years. Why?

Has the value you provide to your clients decreased? Do you have so little confidence in your value and differentiation that even asking for a 1% increase is too much? Is it surprising many agencies are under-performing profitability-wise?

Is it fear that holds us back from increasing our fees each year?

How much is your fear costing you?

If the costs of running a business (i.e. your agency) are increasing, salaries are increasing and you aren't increasing your prices, then profitability is likely to decrease unless you've found ways to be substantially more efficient and productive – that's basic 'school-level' economics.

A senior director in an agency told me proudly they had not increased fees to one of their major clients for eight years. When challenged by me, her response was, "We are still making good money from them."

I think she is missing the point. The agency could have been making more money. The point is that the agency team had received several pay-rises during those eight years. The point is that agency profitability is declining rapidly.

If an agency doesn't increase its fees to a client long term, what signal does that send to the client?

Mistake 6: Lack of meaningful differentiation

Understandably, clients try to commoditise an agency's work and then compare its price to that of its competitors. Unfortunately, many agencies also commoditise themselves by having no meaningful differentiation or distinctiveness.

Being 'results focused, highly creative, passionate and great people' is no longer a differentiator for an agency! These are clichés used by many agencies.

Not surprisingly, clients and customers do not want to pay more money if there is no discernible difference between two products or services.

If there is a difference, is it significant and important enough for the client to be prepared to pay more? If so, how much more will they pay? How valuable is that difference to the client?

Clients encourage agencies to think they buy their services simply on price. Clients, and increasingly Procurement specialists, ask about the hourly and daily rates for different levels of people so they can compare like with like.

It is hard work to find ways to differentiate your services, especially in ways that your clients care about. But the hard work is worth it.

How distinctive is your agency or service? Will clients pay a premium for your services?

The more agencies are commoditised, the less money they will make. Fact.

Mistake 7: Tolerating clients that are unprofitable

Are you working with clients that have become increasingly unprofitable over time?

Or was the business won when the agency lacked confidence to charge a higher price?

Or is your client continuously challenging your prices? Or maybe all three?

These unprofitable clients are often held onto because they are seen as an important contributor to turnover or they are seen as 'important clients/names.' How many 'trophy' clients can an agency afford?

The problem is that these unprofitable clients also suck out agency resource which could have been deployed on winning, and working with, more profitable clients. My name for these clients is the 'profit vampires.' They suck out profitability. Identify them and decide what action to take. How many of your agency's clients are profit vampires?

It is rumoured that one of the most successful management consultancies culls its bottom 5% of under-performing clients each year. Should you consider that approach? You need to replace them with more profitable clients.

Do you believe that price is the be all and end all? Do you think the client will make up their mind based solely on your price? This mindset is dangerous, affecting our demeanour, our conversation, our questions, even our creative ideas. This, coupled with a sense of desperation, leads to submitting cheap prices, reduced self-esteem and a 'run faster/do, do, do' mentality.

Some years ago, an agency colleague of mine resigned a major corporate client, a famous fizzy drinks company. We were losing money despite winning more than our fair share of pitches.

The client refused to allow us to increase our fee rates or reduce the number of agencies on their roster. In the end we decided to resign the client.

The client responded to my colleague saying, "You can't resign us, we are xyz fizzy drinks company."

We still resigned the client! It's your choice.

Ask yourself: if business was booming with lots of work coming in from both existing and new clients and you could afford to resign one or two of your unprofitable/least profitable clients, which client(s) would you resign?

Mistake 8: Over-dependence

I ask my agency clients what percentage of their revenue and/or profitability comes from their top three clients. I am surprised how often the top three clients account for 60 % and sometimes even as high as 80 % to 90 % of their revenue. If this is the case, it is likely the top three clients represent an even greater proportion of the agency's profitability.

When I probe more deeply, I am surprised how often I find their top client is 40-50 % of the business. In this situation it is difficult to have a healthy, balanced business relationship.

Some venture capitalists believe no client should represent more than 15 - 20 % of the business and the top six clients no more than 60 % of the business.

Client-agency relationships which are out of balance produce poor work, become increasingly unprofitable over time and are rarely satisfying or motivating for the agency. Neither side respects the other and they may even end up resenting each other. Even if the relationship does last a long time, often the self-confidence of the agency will have been eroded.

Nigel Bogle, one of the founders of BBH (Bartle Bogle Hegarty), a leading UK advertising agency, says, "We're only **three** phone calls away from disaster."

Does this need to be adjusted for those agencies where the main client is over 40% of the business to 'We're only <u>one</u> phone call away from disaster?'

How many phone calls away from disaster is your agency?

Mistake 9: Chasing after increasingly smaller opportunities

As you chase more opportunities, so those opportunities tend to be smaller pieces of business.

During tough economic times, as the pressure increases to maintain or achieve high returns, many agencies simply chase more opportunities with lower budgets, run even faster and fail to sell real value.

It is so easy in desperation to chase after increasingly smaller pieces of business with dwindling levels of return. When we chase these smaller opportunities, often our self-belief and confidence decline. We also exhaust the senior team, pursuing small opportunities which are unlikely to be profitable and put unnecessary pressure on resources.

When you chase two monkeys both will escape.
Chinese proverb

Mistake 10: Accepting poor or inadequate briefs

When we accept verbal briefs from clients, or poorly thought through briefs, there is a risk when we respond. Verbal briefs allow too much 'wiggle-room' and the opportunity to ramble and change your mind over time. Written briefs force the client to focus and prioritise their requirements.

Those briefs with no budget or budget guideline are also risky. Those with unrealistic expectations are likely to result in disappointment – either for the client, the agency, or both.

Has the brief been approved at a senior level? Has the budget been assigned? Do you have a reasonable chance of winning? (You define 'reasonable.')

You can waste so much time going off in the wrong direction or focusing on the wrong aspect of the brief. Or, annoyingly, refining a proposal which, when you present it to the client, you are told, 'We can't afford that!'

Managing client expectations is a vital skill that typically comes with experience. Remember the old adage:

Under-promise and over-deliver.

Mistake 11: Presenting budgets to clients which are unprofitable to you or pitching your price too low

A lack of confidence in the value that the agency provides can lead to decreasing confidence and a downward financial spiral.

This can be the result of aggressive competition, either perceived or real. Or the lack of confidence can be when the agency is on the back foot, perhaps during a re-pitch or after poor work/results have been delivered, or a new senior client contact puts pressure on prices or questions every price.

An MD of an agency was telling me about a new business pitch they had recently made. He told me proudly, "We priced it to win." I asked, "What does that mean?" He frowned, thought for a few moments and, looking despondent, said, "We under-priced it."

Mark Ritson, Associate Professor of Marketing at London Business School reckons that:

'Most companies' pricing strategy is a mixture of voodoo and bingo.'

Mistake 12: Falling for clients' lies

Has a client lied to you? What was the cost?

Clients tell lies. Clients use a number of classic lies in their negotiations with their agency. One of my all-time favourites is:

'I have two identical proposals which are both substantially cheaper than yours.'

This is a complete lie. If they really had two **identical** proposals which are cheaper, why would they bother talking to you? They would simply buy from one of the other providers. What they mean is **similar** proposals which are cheaper but inferior in some way.

Another common lie is:

> *'Just give me a ball-park, I won't hold you to it.'*

Beware: they will hold you to it!

> *'Do this first job at a special introductory price and I have lots more work in the future.'*

They infer your rate will return to 'normal' after this first job. Another lie.

Do they lie deliberately? Probably not. Regardless of whether they are deliberate or not, client lies will impact your profitability.

What client lies have you fallen for?

Mistake 13: Short-term generosity becoming long-term obligations

What favours for clients have you later regretted?

We provide some extra work or something of value as a short-term goodwill gesture, often intended by us to be a one-off favour. For a variety of reasons, the gesture then becomes expected in the future by the client or it becomes awkward for us to withdraw the favour.

As this 'gesture' continues and is repeated, it then becomes an established precedent which becomes 'the accepted norm' and is now difficult to stop.

We wish we had never made the gesture in the first place.

What precedents do you wish you could reverse?

Mistake 14: Lacking negotiation expertise

At the start of a negotiation workshop I sometimes ask how many of the participants have been on a negotiation workshop before.

For agencies, the typical answer is the minority, perhaps 10 %. I then ask how many of the agency's clients do they think have received negotiation training; the answer is 'the vast majority' or 'all of them.'

This imbalance and ignorance of the key principles of negotiation among many agency personnel leads to fees being presented by agencies which are too low, agency profitability shrinking year on year and the agency scared to push back for fear of rocking the boat.

We fall into the mistaken belief that the only way to negotiate is simply one of two extremes: either to just give in to the other party's demands or play 'hard-ball' and demand what you want, give nothing and don't move an inch.

Very occasionally, I meet agencies that tell me their senior team do all the negotiations and the rest of their people don't really do much negotiating. I believe they are mistaken. This pre-supposes that the only real negotiation is around high-level fees and rates.

We negotiate all the time, every day, with clients.

Negotiation comes into play in a variety of areas on a day-to-day basis, far beyond simply agreeing fee levels: from the quality of the client-agency relationship, the quality of the brief, presenting and selling creative work, agreeing timings, deadlines and the urgency for work, changes to the scope of work or specifications and so on.

In fact, negotiation comes into nearly every area of agency client management.

It is a fundamental part of a relationship with clients, both day-to-day and long term. It applies at all levels throughout the agency.

If you think the cost of training and education is expensive then wait till you discover that ignorance costs even more.

My agency clients tell me the cost of our negotiation workshop typically pays for itself within a few weeks. That is an excellent Return on Investment.

Then we come to probably one of the biggest and most costly mistakes for agencies and many other service businesses...

Mistake 15: Scope creep

How much is scope creep costing you?

The client keeps pushing for more and more to be done within the existing budget and scope of work. These extras, over and above the original scope of work, are somehow expected to be done for free and included within the original price.

Scope creep is like a disease. It is contagious. The longer it is left unchecked, the harder it is to stop or reverse.

Several agency directors have told me they reckon that scope creep is costing their agency at least 20% of their profits each year.

I suspect that much scope creep often goes on within agencies unknown to senior management, as anxious account handlers don't want to rock the boat and find it hard to say 'no.'

Scope creep becomes a form of death by a thousand cuts.

How much do your people give away without senior management knowledge or approval?

Stop making these mistakes

How frustrating these mistakes are. You can see how easily these mistakes are to make. The easy answer is simply to work even longer hours, run faster and faster, keep doing what you are doing and not bother to learn to negotiate.

How many of these different negotiation mistakes have you made in the past 12 months?

Mistake 1: Price crumbling

Mistake 2: Lack of preparation

Mistake 3: Thinking great 'client service' is always saying 'yes'

Mistake 4: Pressure can lead to wrong decisions

Mistake 5: Not increasing fees and rates

Mistake 6: Lack of meaningful differentiation

Mistake 7: Tolerating clients that are unprofitable

Mistake 8: Over-dependence

Mistake 9: Chasing after increasingly smaller opportunities

Mistake 10: Accepting poor or inadequate briefs

Mistake 11: Presenting budgets to clients which are unprofitable to you or pitching your price too low

Mistake 12: Falling for clients' lies

Mistake 13: Short-term generosity becoming long-term obligations

Mistake 14: Lacking negotiation expertise

Mistake 15: Scope creep

How many of these mistakes do you expect to make in the coming 12 months?

How much are these mistakes costing your agency, your confidence and your relationships with your clients?

How much more profit could your agency be making whilst improving your client-agency relationship?

*Why do **smart** people make such **stupid** mistakes?* is a book designed to help you make more informed choices, choose your responses and then work smarter. You can be more profitable, whilst delivering huge quantities of value to your client and building stronger client-agency relationships. Value which takes your client's business closer to achieving their critical business goals and, in so doing, will take you closer to achieving your business goals.

The next chapter will outline the key principles of negotiation that will help you avoid some of the mistakes featured in this chapter.

CHAPTER 2

Negotiation principles

Key points in this chapter

- The main negotiation principles

- The four steps of negotiating

- A framework when planning a negotiation

Great client service isn't always saying 'yes'.
How much is your 'yes' costing you?

So what is negotiating? There are various long textbook definitions for 'negotiations' which touch on 'the resolution of conflict... between two opposing parties... to arrive at a mutually satisfactory result...'

Wikipedia defines Negotiation as *'a dialogue intended to resolve disputes, to produce an agreement upon courses of action, to bargain for individual or collective advantage, or to craft outcomes to satisfy various interests.'*

My definition in the context of agencies is:

Getting more of what you want whilst maintaining, or even developing, the relationship, then balancing commercial judgement with human nature.

If you get what you want but the other party feels unfairly treated or that they have a poor deal, there is a likelihood they may walk away from the deal or plan revenge at a later date.

We then need to take account of the commercial realities of your position financially and the marketplace, balanced against the likely reaction of the other party; people respond differently.

This definition is particularly relevant where you have an ongoing relationship with a client; it is less relevant to a single one-off transaction.

We negotiate all the time – we just don't realise. The ability to negotiate is like a muscle: it requires regular exercise, it needs to develop and strengthen slowly and, as your confidence grows, so it can be used more.

Why are negotiation skills important for everyone but especially for advisers, consultants, sales people and for those working in agencies?

1. **Clients want more for less.** Clients are trying to squeeze every last drop from their (often reduced) budgets.

2. **Agency profitability has reduced.** The profitability of most agencies, and many companies, is under immense pressure. The traditional business model for an agency is becoming increasingly hard to generate a decent return on investment.

3. **Competition has increased and supply exceeds demand.** There is always another agency willing to work for less. In tough times, this competition becomes even more cut-throat. Clients can be tempted to take the (perceived) lowest cost option.

4. **Client service people, it seems, are genetically wired to say 'yes'** – saying 'no' goes against the grain. A 'can-do attitude' is a great attribute and appeals to clients considering appointing an agency but it can lead you to agree fees, timings and activity which are not in your best interest long term.

5. **The buyer has all the power.** A common misconception is that the party with the budget or the cheque-book wields most or all of the power. Not necessarily. The best business relationships are in balance; each party contributes and each party feels they are receiving a fair return and rates the relationship as 'highly satisfying.' Those clients who simply abuse their position as the buyer will not get the best work in the long term.

6. **Many services provided by agencies have been 'de-mystified'.** The 'black-art' of many agency services has been unveiled. Clients believe, rightly or wrongly, that they are able to develop some campaigns themselves without an agency's involvement. In fact, we have increasingly seen clients able to produce award-winning campaigns without help from a traditional agency.

7. **Buyer-supplier or peer-to-peer partnership?** The type of relationship between the adviser and their client will dramatically affect the quality of work and output. I consistently produce my best work with clients who share their plans, value my input and expertise and respect my opinion. Too frequently, agencies tell me that they are experiencing a 'master-slave' relationship or 'buyer-supplier' relationship with their clients. Unfortunately, these clients are often the 'big names,' the trusted brands on the high street.

8.**Procurement departments and professional buyers.** Major companies like British Airways and Diageo have invested in the area of Procurement. These professional buyers vary in their understanding of marketing services and marketing communication and can sometimes use powerful negotiation techniques aggressively to reduce prices and agency profitability.

Some Procurement specialists have helped make some important improvements for agencies such as improved briefs, improved processes and fairer agency remuneration.

However, the malpractice by some Procurement 'professionals,' often not spoken of publicly for fear of retribution, is far too common and is a disgrace to the profession of Procurement and to the companies employing them.

9. **Most clients are better trained to negotiate than their agencies.** Major corporate clients are trained regularly in how to negotiate; most agency people are not. This puts agencies at a distinct disadvantage.

10. **Commoditisation.** There is an increasing danger of commoditisation within many industries. True differentiation and distinctiveness between agencies is harder to achieve as most differentiators are easily replicated by competitors. The more agencies allow themselves to be commoditised, the less profitable they will be. One of the most powerful differentiators in agencies is the agency's people. Their relationship with their clients can be an important reason why a client appoints and retains a particular agency.

The Four Steps of Negotiation

There are four key steps in negotiation:

- Prepare

- Open

- Bargain

- Close

These are not always totally discrete and can merge, especially in a quick negotiation.

However, there are specific issues and considerations within each of the four steps.

Prepare: In a nutshell, this is about getting your 'ducks in order.' It can be formal planning or simply taking time to stop and think. This step involves gathering information, understanding what is valuable to both parties, clarifying what it is that you want, choosing your mindset and how you will go about the negotiation. Anticipation of how the other party may react to your approach is helpful. In our negotiation workshop we spend as much time on preparation as on the other three steps put together.

Open: This is a key time to influence the other party. Everything from your body language, your opening words, your questions, your confidence and demeanour will affect the quality of your opening and their likely reaction. This is when you expose to the other party what it is that you want. Whatever your opening position, you need to have a reason for why you are proposing it. You need to articulate it clearly, concisely and confidently.

Bargain: This is the classic perception of 'negotiating' – the 'to and fro' nature of the bazaar or market-stall. Each move you make should be planned rather than a knee-jerk reaction to what they say or do. Your ability to ask high-quality questions, manage and even pre-empt their objections and your listening skills will be vital tools in achieving your goal. Trading is a crucial skill to be employed during this stage. High-quality questions can give you time to think, help you gather valuable information and also demonstrate your expertise and confidence.

Close: Generally, the close should be straightforward if you have prepared, opened and bargained well. However, the close can be fraught with danger. Last-minute tricks can be employed. Our urgency to close the deal can lead to giving away unplanned valuable concessions at the last minute. Often we are far more aware of our deadlines than the other party. In the best negotiations, both parties leave satisfied and feeling they have achieved the best deal for their requirements and situation.

Key principles

There are a number of negotiation principles that will help you achieve your goal. Many are relevant during all four key steps; however, they tend to sit neatly with, and are more relevant to, one of the four steps.

Prepare

Prepare 1. Spend time on your preparation. This gives you confidence and increases your likelihood of achieving your goal. The relatively small amount of time spent on your preparation will provide a huge return on investment. It is common when we are under pressure to skip the preparation only to regret it later in the meeting or negotiation.

There are few areas in life where preparation pays off more than in negotiations.

When you prepare properly you will have more time to observe the body language of the other party, listen actively to what is being said and to think through and plan your response. Your preparation means you can concentrate much more on the other party, their requirements and their level of confidence.

> **Plans are nothing. Planning is everything.**
> Dwight D Eisenhower

Prepare 2. Aim realistically high. When you are selling, it is much easier to come down in price than it is to go up in price. In the long run, those who aim higher do better; however, you will need to have reasons for the level of your fee or price. If you aim too high it can be counter-productive. Price levels do also suggest quality levels; a higher price is generally associated with higher quality. We expect to pay more for a Mont Blanc pen, a Rolex watch, a fillet steak. Leave yourself room to negotiate.

Fear can play an important part in how high we aim. It can prevent us aiming high. F.E.A.R. stands for **F**alse **E**xpectations **A**ppearing **R**eal. Most of our fears are rarely as bad as we expected. So aim high, but realistically high. Some take this to extremes!

> **If you want a hamster aim for a pony!**
> Amelia, aged 8

This is probably too extreme in the business context but demonstrates clearly the emotional leverage in relationships.

Prepare 3. Plan your ideal, target and walk-away. Have three different price levels in your mind: your **ideal** which you will be thrilled if accepted; your **target** which you will be happy with; and your **walk-away** which is the point at which we say 'no.' You may decide to attach different conditions and concessions to each price level. If you go into a negotiation with just one figure in your mind, you are more likely to be put on the back foot and start dropping your price and/or more likely to become emotionally intransigent and unable to move on price.

The other reason I am keen on three different price levels is that it gives your client options and choice. Choice enables them to feel more in control.

The walk-away price is particularly important. It can save you agreeing to a deal which you later regret. Curiously, the act of walking away – whether in reality or metaphorically – often causes the other party to soften their position and concede to you.

A walk-away is particularly important in an e-auction. It is easy to get carried away in the moment.

You can also prepare an 'alternative position.' This is a different approach to offer the other party if all else is failing.

Prepare 4. Get their shopping list. Understanding what is of value to the other party and what their priorities are will prove to be very useful. As a diligent adviser to your clients, you should be asking them insightful questions about the outcomes they require, what would be really valuable to them and what they have had previously that was particularly useful. This helps you achieve greater clarity over how they define value. If you are able to ask the client to prioritise their shopping list then this will be even better. Simply ask, "Which of these factors is most important to you?" And then, "Which is next most important? What is really valuable to you? Why is that?" These very simple questions will enable you to provide a more on-target proposal which is more likely to be bought by the client, everything else being equal.

Prepare 5. Your state and level of confidence. In advance of a negotiation, think how you can be in the right state and your confidence at the appropriate level. Many of us don't bother; we simply turn up and hope for the best. Confidence in your position, your value and yourself is vital. The other party will very quickly pick up your confidence level. We like to buy from people who are confident. Nervousness will put clients off from choosing you and your proposal. Your confidence enables the client to feel confident in their decision to buy from you. The right level of confidence is important. Too much confidence can come across as arrogance which will repel clients; the right level will feel congruent, natural and authentic.

Prepare 6. Plan your/their concessions in order of priority. By considering everything on your wish list and their shopping list you can then prioritise them accordingly. Understand what is not negotiable, what are your 'must-haves,' 'like to haves,' 'can't haves' and non-negotiables. What issues are you unable to compromise on under virtually any circumstance? The value of concessions can easily be under-estimated, yet they can be immensely valuable. The best concessions the client can offer you are those which have a high value to you and low cost to the other party. The best concessions you can offer the other party are high value to them and low cost to you.

Client
High value

Agency
High value

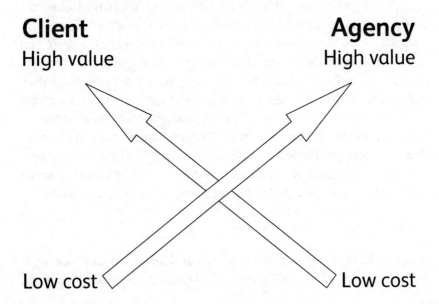

Low cost

Low cost

For example, early payment terms may have high value to the agency especially if cash flow is poor. Yet for many marketing clients, whether they pay now or in three months' time has no impact on their overall budget.

Prepare 7. Precedents. Can be very dangerous and can commit you for the long term to something you originally offered as a one-off.

> *A short-term act of generosity, which becomes a long-term obligation.*

Think into the future. What might I be committing myself or my company to for the foreseeable future?

> *Imagine you and your partner visit a local new Italian restaurant run by Luigi to celebrate an important anniversary for you both. You have a wonderful meal, great wine, great service, great conversation and great atmosphere. When you ask for the bill, Luigi also brings two complimentary glasses of brandy 'on the house.' This is a lovely gesture which is the finishing touch to a great evening.*

> *A month or so later you have another important celebration (perhaps to celebrate the results of your new negotiation skills?) and decide to return to Luigi's restaurant. Again you have a wonderful meal, great wine, great service, great conversation and great atmosphere. You ask Luigi for the bill. He brings only the bill. What else are you expecting? Two glasses of brandy perhaps? Luigi has set a precedent. You now expect the brandy each time you visit his restaurant. Your likelihood to return has now reduced, yet everything else (a wonderful meal, great wine, great service, great conversation and great atmosphere) remained the same.*

> *So unless Luigi intends to give a free glass of brandy to each customer every time, what should Luigi have done to avoid this expectation in the future? He needs to give a 'condition.'*

Luigi could say, "This is our first week of opening our restaurant and, to celebrate, I'd like to offer you both a complimentary glass of brandy," or

"I believe this is your first visit to my restaurant. Can I offer you both a complimentary glass of brandy to celebrate this first visit?"

How often have you provided some extra value to a client as a short-term gesture and it has then become expected by that client every time in the future? So in future, as part of your preparation and planning, ask yourself, 'What precedents might I be setting for the future?' Precedents can sometimes sneak up slowly on you. They become more and more established and more and more expected. When that happens, the gesture becomes very hard to stop.

An agency client was telling me how their 'soft drinks client,' after a meeting at the agency's office, asked the agency if they could continue to use the boardroom for their own internal meeting. "Sure," the agency said, "can I get you more coffee?" What's wrong with that? Nothing – yet.

However, a few weeks later the soft drinks company phoned the agency to book the agency's boardroom for an 'away-day.' "Sure," said the agency, "What do we need to do to prepare for the away-day?"

"Nothing," said the client, "It's just for us internally, you aren't involved."

When the day came, the client kept the junior account executive occupied all day with requests for more coffee and tea, photocopying and various other tasks.

A month later the client rang again asking to book the agency's boardroom. At what point do you put your foot down and politely say 'no' or say something other than 'yes'? The longer you leave addressing the precedent, the harder it becomes or the bigger an issue it becomes.

Prepare 8. Think about your bottom line. Ensure you are clear in your mind about the implications for your profitability of every negotiation, or at least every major negotiation. Profitability has come under huge pressure in most businesses especially during recent tough economic times. For most client-facing people who are essentially 'selling' to clients, their focus is predominantly on the top line or revenue line – the price we will charge the client. We must also understand how the revenue translates into profit.

All clients must be profitable unless there is a specific strategic reason, such as you want to develop a particular expertise, to raise your profile working with a particular client or in a particular sector or there is greater potential longer term.

If your agency works on 10% profit on revenue earned, then every 1% more revenue without increasing other costs increases your profits by 10%. So if you can negotiate an extra 1% revenue, this cascades as 10% onto your bottom line. A corresponding 1% reduction in negotiated revenue will reduce your profitability by 10%. By good negotiation you can achieve much more than a 1% improvement in revenue.

This is the ultimate in 'working smarter, not harder.'

Rafi Mohammed in his book The Art of Pricing explains that a study of 27 different industry sectors, from retail to IT to banking to travel, found on average that:

1% increase in average price typically leads to an 11% increase in operating profit; conversely,

1% decrease in average price typically leads to an 11% decrease in operating profit.

Recent work in 2010 by McKinsey has found a similar relationship. They found that each 1% increase in price typically leads to a 9.7% increase in profitability. (Perhaps the small difference between the 11% and the 9.7% is due to reducing profitability for many businesses during the recession).

Profitability for many agencies is on a knife-edge. It is therefore vital to understand the impact of each decision you make on your agency's profitability.

> *Small change, big impact.*
> *Small change on the top line, big impact on the bottom line.*

Prepare 9. Put yourself in their shoes. Great negotiators take time to see the deal from the other party's perspective. This often affects your language and thinking, enabling a resolution to be achieved more easily. Take time to actually see the deal from the other party's perspective. Imagine you are the other party. What is important to you? What is a 'must have?' How do you see 'you?'

> *If there is any great secret of success in life,*
> *it lies in the ability to put yourself in the other person's place*
> *and to see things from his point of view.* Henry Ford

Prepare 10. Test the water. Don't leave all the negotiating to the negotiation meeting. See if you can sow seeds to manage or change the other party's expectations.

For example, you could say to a client, "How do you see your requirements for next year? We have been looking ahead and we may need to make some changes to the team and/or fee levels." The client's response will give you useful clues as to their receptiveness to an increase in fee or change in the team members. Turn up your 'antennae' to full sensitivity, watching for little clues, body language changes and flinches made by your client.

Prepare 11. Fast preparation. If you have very little time to prepare then at least consider the following:

- Your 'wants' or 'must haves' in order of priority

- Plan your opening offer and opening remarks

- Decide your walk-away position

- Be prepared to say 'no'

- Plan your concessions and your wish list

- Aim for win-win

- Be ready to give yourself time to think

- Can authority, or absence of authority, be used to good effect? ('My board insist on xyz')

- Consider what options are available to give the other party choice

Open

Opening is what you initially put on the table as a price, budget or requirements. It is a key time to influence the other party.

Open 1: Set the agenda. Take control of the meeting without taking over. Lead and guide the meeting. Ensure you control the order of topics for discussion.

Open 2: If you don't ask, you don't get. You cannot afford to be timid and passive. You are in 'sales' and as such need to be assertive. You may not always get what you want by asking but you have a much higher chance if you do at least ask.

Open 3: Open first or second? Intuitively we think it is better to open first. Most of the research and my experience suggest that in the majority of situations it is better to open second. However, it is not a black and white issue. There is a school of thought that recommends opening first. What are the arguments for and against each?

	Opening first	Opening second
Arguments for	Straight away gives a strong assertive confident position. May influence the other party to moderate their position.	By opening second you can see more clearly what it is that the other party wants and what is most important to them. 'The longer you take to say your price the more money you will make.'
Arguments against	You may miss out on opportunities to have asked for more. The other party may avoid their opening and simply 'attack' your opening position. 'The sooner you say your price, the less money you will make.'	Because you are opening second you may be influenced to moderate your opening. If you moderately reduce your price, that may be bad. If you moderately increase your price because of something said by the other party in their opening, that could be good. You may appear hesitant and lacking in self-belief.

As you can see, it is not a clear-cut decision. You must decide each time whether to open first or second. Generally, I recommend agencies to open second. The reason for this is that by opening second you have a clearer understanding of your client's requirements, are more able to take a consultative approach to solving their problems and you can ask high-quality questions that can demonstrate your expertise and differentiation from your competitors.

Open 4: Create an aura of expertise. From an early stage in the client-agency relationship, demonstrate your expertise in your given subject(s). Do it without coming across as a 'know-all.' Clients often employ external advisers and agencies to solve their problems. See yourself as a 'problem-solver and profit-improver' for your clients. Prepare your questions in advance. The quality of your questions can show your expertise. You don't need to provide all the answers at the early stage, just show your understanding of your client's business.

During tough times, like the recession, it seems that expertise becomes even more important. It's not simply lower prices that people want but certainty in the result they will enjoy and that they are making the right choice. They want risk reduction. Making a wrong decision in a recession is more costly than when times are better because budgets are more limited, jobs are less secure and results are more carefully analysed under the microscope.

Risk Reduction becomes more important than Price Reduction.

Open 5: Anticipate their likely opening, questions and objections. Put yourself in their shoes. What would you do? What would be your likely approach? How would 'you' put pressure on 'you?' What questions would 'you' ask 'you?' What objections would 'you' throw at 'you?'

Anticipate their likely openings and plan how you should respond in each case.

Open 6: Don't argue, ask questions. The typical reaction when our price is challenged or we are put under pressure in a negotiation is to argue our point of view. The risk with this response is that we appear defensive **and** emotional. Arguing tends to make both parties dig in, become more intransigent and less likely to be flexible and give you what you want. Instead, ask well planned, well constructed questions, then listen carefully and actively. This is a far more influential way to understand the other party's thought processes.

This gives you more time to think, gain useful information and gauge the other party's level of determination. When you ask questions and listen, you are in control.

For example, your client tells you they think your fees are very expensive. Often our first reaction is to argue defensively with the client that our fees represent good value for money and are in line with market rates. Often in this situation neither party will change their opinion.

However, if you ask questions, firstly you will find out the reasons for the client's statement and secondly you will be more likely to influence their thinking to change towards your position. For example, 'What makes you say that we are expensive? What are you comparing us to? What will be the value to you of getting this project right? How much extra value, sales, new customers, profit or market share is this likely to create? What will that be worth to you?'

I have also found from personal experience that this approach keeps the conversation calmer and less confrontational.

Open 7: Talk less, listen more. Listen carefully to the other party. Don't interrupt. Hear their full point of view. Restate their point of view to show you understand. We learn nothing when we are talking and learn so much when we listening. A trap that is easy to fall into for agency and sales people is to talk too much, especially about what we know well: ourselves, our agency and our proposal. As a rule of thumb, you should talk 30-40% and your client 60-70%, especially during fact-finding and briefing.

Bargain

Bargain 1: Seek Win-Win. This maintains the relationship. Do this by trading and seeking high satisfaction for both parties. Aim for both parties to be highly satisfied.

Bargain 2: Trade. Don't give things (money, concessions or tradables) away; trade them or swap them for other concessions. So if a client asks for a discount then swap the discount for something else of value to you. This can be very powerful when you ask for something that is highly valuable to you but has little cost to the other party.

When you give valuable things away without trading them, there is a strong possibility that the other party either sees what you've given away as lacking much value or that you are making so much money that you can afford to give away so much – or worse, both. This simply makes them want more from you.

A good phrase to use when trading is:

If you..... then I ......

'**If you** pay in advance and agree to a three-month notice period **then I** can give you a 3 % discount.'

The order is important. In the sentence above it is a statement. If you reverse it to **If I do .... will you do....?** It then becomes a closed question and has more likelihood of the client saying 'no.' For example, 'If I give you a 3 % discount, then will you agree to pay in advance and agree to a three-month notice period?'

Trading concessions also reduces the likelihood of the client 'price-nibbling' and asking for lots of extras.

Does this mean that you should never do anything over and above your scope of work for clients? Isn't going the extra mile right? It is fine to provide small concessions or actions which are valuable to your client to show your commitment. However, think into the future about what implications this may have longer term. Beware of setting precedents which can quickly become expected. Very quickly the 'extra' becomes seen as the norm.

Bargain 3: Wish list. Develop a wish list of tradable items. These are items which are valuable to you and relatively low cost to the other party. There is no right or wrong as to what goes on the wish list; it depends on what's valuable to you. So if your cash-flow is poor then upfront or early payment terms will be a real priority on your wish list.

Your wish list might include such tradables as:

- Payment terms

- Introductions and referrals

- Case studies

- Testimonials

In my negotiation workshops I work with agencies to develop their own wish lists, often with a dozen or more tradables.

Bargain 4: Wish lists for your agency and also a tailored wish list for each individual client. I recommend developing a wish list for your company which is consulted prior to all negotiation discussions. Then tailor it to each individual client company as there are different opportunities and concessions within each client company.

Bargain 5: Negotiated money is the fastest money you will ever make or lose.

Would you like to earn the equivalent of £360,000/hour?

Let's imagine you are negotiating a retainer fee with a client of £24,000/month. The client then pressurises you to drop the fee. You agree to reduce the fee by £1,000/month. How long did it take you to drop the fee by £1,000/month – one minute, two minutes? Let's say two minutes, that's equivalent to losing £360,000 in an hour (£1,000 x 12 months x 60/2 minutes). Imagine the reverse situation where you negotiate an increase in your retainer fee – you can earn the equivalent of £360,000/hour for two minutes' work. Can you see the potential impact that skilful and effective negotiating can have on your business's profitability?

Bargain 6: Authority is a powerful tool. Authority can be used in a variety of ways. One way is to intimidate you. This is where the client's boss or Managing Director enters your meeting at the client's offices and, on being introduced to you, tells you he can't believe how much your agency's rates and fees are. This is often simply to put pressure on you to believe 'their MD thinks we are really expensive.'

'Absent authority' can also be used against you. This is when a client explains to you that their boss thinks your fee is very expensive and that their boss says they will only hire you if you reduce your fee. The client will sometimes then tell you how <u>they</u> think your fee proposal is very fair. This is a form of 'good cop, bad cop.' You have to judge whether this is real or fictitious. One way to call their bluff is to ask to meet with the boss to discuss the project and the fee level. If they are reluctant, then position the meeting as you and your day-to-day client contact working together to present an important initiative to their boss.

You can use 'absent authority' in reverse to your benefit. When you are under pressure to reduce your fee you can explain that, unfortunately, your board will not agree to a reduction. (I suggest that the 'absent authority' is an amorphous group, e.g. the board or senior management, rather than a specific individual such as your boss or your MD, as there is a possibility your client may demand that they talk on the phone immediately to 'your boss'.)

Bargain 7: Keep the whole deal in mind. Negotiations can become quite emotional. One specific topic may derail a negotiation. In this situation, it is possible to lose sight of the bigger picture of the whole deal and become hung-up on a minor issue. Remind yourself what the overall big picture is. What is your ultimate goal from this negotiation?

Bargain 8: Always have a BATNA. Negotiation text-books talk about a 'BATNA' – the Best Alternative To a Negotiated Agreement. This means: what alternative do you have if you don't reach agreement?

The best way to see how this is important is to imagine a client demanding a 25% reduction in fee immediately with no reduction in team or input. If the client accounts for 40-50% of your business, you have very little choice about how you can respond. You are possibly going to agree to their demands or, at best, a reduced level; whereas if the client accounts for only 10% of your business, you have a BATNA. You have choices which include refusing, trading, compromising or even resigning the client. These options give you more power to negotiate. Always give yourself choices – avoid a *fait accompli* situation. You always want to have a BATNA.

Bargain 9: Give yourself time to think. When we are under pressure in a meeting to negotiate, or more likely agree to a client's proposed fee reduction, there is a risk that we agree to a particular term and then subsequently regret our decision. Do not simply agree because you feel under pressure. If you are going to agree to a revised term or price then make sure you have had time to think through the implications for your business. Simple phrases can buy you time so you can consider the decision in your own time without the immediate pressure, for example:

'I need time to review the numbers again.'

'I will need to discuss this with my board.'

'I need some time to think this through, the implications are too important to rush the decision.'

'I need to sleep on this.'

Even a simple comfort break can give you a few minutes to think in an unpressured environment.

Bargain 10: Let them work for every concession. When we negotiate, if we have had to work hard for the deal, typically we feel we have got a better deal. If we agree a deal too easily, there is a likelihood that the other party thinks they have not asked for enough and there is more available to negotiate – all they have to do is come back to the negotiation table and push.

'Slice the salami thin' – if you reduce your price, do so in very small increments. This helps to manage the client's expectations to expect less of a reduction. The smaller the amount you come down in price, the more the other party will assume there is less room for you to manoeuvre.

Bargain 11: Give options. When you provide options to your client, this seems to have the effect that the other party feels more in control because they have a choice. Work done by Harvard Business School found that no more than three options should be provided. The three different options can be trimmed-down versions of the same proposal with three different price structures, or the three options can be three completely different proposals, such as:

1. One safe route/on budget.

2. One slightly risky and slightly over budget.

3. One more risky and over budget.

Bargain 12: Plan and use your great responses to tough statements and questions. There are various statements and questions you can use which, at minimum, give you more time to think and, in some cases, can persuade a client to come around to your view.

'On what basis is it too expensive?'

'Why do you think that other agency has dropped their fee so much?'

Close

Close 1: No deal is better than a bad deal. It is difficult to turn down a deal, even a bad deal, and sometimes we can be tempted to agree a deal that, long term, has poor consequences for us and our agency. We must be able to recognise a situation when we are better off declining the deal and even walking away. The alternative is to agree the deal and then discover it is unprofitable, demands too much resource and time or other negative results for us.

It seems many sales people and agency people are unable to walk away from a deal, no matter how poor the deal is for them.

Close 2: The winner's curse. When a deal is agreed too quickly or too easily, there is a risk that either party – or even both parties – suffers from the 'winner's curse.' This is the feeling that although you've agreed the deal you could and should have done a better deal. There is a risk that one party tries to renege on the agreed deal.

It seems that to avoid this feeling it is preferable to have had some movement in the deal, some sense of haggling and trading.

Close 3: Time pressure to close the deal. It is often at the end of a negotiation that we tend to give away the most concessions in our anxiousness to close the deal. Some negotiation experts believe that as much as 90% of the value of the concessions given away is given away in the last 10% of the negotiation time.

It is common in property negotiations for large sums of money to be re-negotiated just before exchange of contracts. Don't be pressured into decisions you may regret later.

This is more likely to happen when we have no alternative options or choice.

Close 4: It's not all over till the ink is dry. Beware of relaxing too much before the contract is signed by both parties. I have seen several situations where the agency thinks the deal is done and the business awarded. The client then slips in a few extra requirements. These have ranged from:

- A reduced monthly fee till their new financial year as the client has supposedly over-spent their budget

- A last-minute extra project that needs to be included within the budget

- The budget is reduced but the results and outputs are to remain as previously agreed

Which is harder to negotiate with: a new client or an existing client?

Generally speaking, with an existing client there are various precedents which have been established over the duration of the relationship. These precedents tend to make it hard to change the methods of working, the rates/prices and the balance of power in the relationship. That doesn't mean it's impossible to negotiate effectively with an existing client; it requires planning and patience.

With new clients, there is an opportunity to start the relationship in the right way by establishing best client-agency practice right from Day One. However, we don't always achieve that 'best practice' from Day One, perhaps because we are excited to have won the new client and we are in the honeymoon phase, or we avoid difficult conversations early on in the relationship thinking we can cover those points further along in the future.

The key principles and techniques outlined in this chapter are vital. However, without the right level of confidence and self-belief they are simply principles and techniques. Your mindset must be in the right place. That's what the next chapter is all about.

CHAPTER 3

A front-foot mindset

Key points in this chapter

- The importance of your mindset on your ability to negotiate

- Some suggestions to help you improve your mindset

- How to move from the back-foot to the front-foot

Pressure leads to wrong decisions.
How well do you and your people respond to client pressure?

A few years ago I was on holiday in Crete with my family and we were driving away in our hire-car from a lovely beach, after a day of swimming and relaxing. My wife said, "There's that man who sold us the honey last year. It was wonderful honey, let's get another jar – no, make that two." My eldest daughter also wanted one and so did my mother. I got out of the car and walked over to the farmer's simple display of honey, bananas and olive oil. The hand-painted sign said 6 euros for each jar of honey. I asked for 4 jars. The farmer said, "24 euros." "Can you give me a discount for four?" I asked.

"Let me explain," he said. "Greek honey is the best honey in the world. Crete honey is the best in Greece and this honey, which is thyme honey, comes from around here and is the best honey in Crete. That makes this the best honey in the world." He took the lid off the jar and I smelt the rich honey.

I handed him the 24 euros and walked away.

What did he do that my clients find so hard to do?

1. He held his price.

2. He understood value and differentiation.

3. He said it with confidence.

How well do you hold your price, understand your value and emanate confidence?

What is a front-foot mindset? A front-foot mindset is where we feel truly confident in the value we provide to our clients, the quality of our work and an inner self-belief in our ability.

Your self-belief and self-confidence are crucial if you are to negotiate successfully and effectively. It seems that clients can detect very quickly what our mindset is.

Are you mainly on the front-foot or back-foot?

What puts us in a back-foot mindset? Unfortunately, it seems easier for most people to go into a back-foot mindset than a front-foot mindset. Typical examples of what pushes us onto the back-foot are:

- Losing existing business

- Losing a new business pitch

- Pressure from overly-aggressive negotiators

- A project going wrong

- A project doesn't deliver as expected or promised

- Even a downturn in the economy

Once you are on the back-foot, a downward spiral can start – we become desperate for business. Then we tend to make poor business decisions, we become more likely to agree to drop our price, more likely to put in low-priced bids, become more dependent on fewer clients, more likely to tolerate abusive client relationships, less able to be creative, less able to spot opportunities and more inclined to seek the safer route.

We find we are saying to ourselves:

'They will never pay that much.'

'The budget isn't that big.'

'The competition will go in with a lower price.'

When we are on the back-foot and in a negative mindset, it also seems we lower our expectations of what we can achieve and we are more likely to attract criticism and complaints from clients who, in turn, become more price-sensitive.

Nigel Bogle of BBH (Bartle Bogle Hegarty, a leading London advertising agency), once said, "**An agency thrives on confidence.**" This is so true of agencies and agency people. It affects virtually every aspect of the agency. It affects new business success, creative output, development of existing clients, retention of key staff, agency profile in the trade press and attracting new employees. Once an agency loses its 'mojo' it is really difficult to reverse the momentum and re-build again.

Over the years, I have seen highly successful agencies move from the front-foot mindset onto the back-foot after losing one or more key clients and/or individual members of the agency team. It seems like a slippery slope. The ability to reverse this downward spiral is not easy. The downward momentum becomes hard to stop and then reverse in order to build it back up again. It seems to be worse in the agency world than in most other professional services such as accountancy, architecture, law and management consultancy. There is a tendency that we drop our prices. We chase after smaller clients and smaller budgets. We say 'yes' without thinking. We become short-term in our thinking.

How many previously successful agencies from the past 20 years no longer exist – excluding those bought by other agencies or the big agency groups? What was the real reason for their demise? How many were too dependent on too few clients?

How do we reverse this downward spiral to get on to a front-foot mindset?

There is no simple answer; it is more about a collection of actions to contribute to re-building confidence.

1. **No client to be over 10-15% of the business.** This enables you to have the option always to walk away without damaging the overall agency business too much. Never forget you have a choice.

   I appreciate there are many very successful agencies who do not adhere to this guideline. However, nothing is forever; twenty years ago, the advertising agency Masius lost Mars who had been a major client for over 60 years – is that a record?

   There are quite a few agencies in the UK where the biggest client accounts for 30 %, 40 % or even 50 % of their revenue. In that situation, I believe that the agency's number one priority is to grow the client base to reduce this dominance from one or two major clients. I see this as even more crucial than improving overall agency profitability. Having a more 'healthy' spread of clients will affect your mindset and enable you to feel more front-foot.

Venture Capitalists have a rule of thumb: the top six clients should be a maximum of 60 % of the business. I would add to this that the top three clients should be no more than 40 % of the business.

2. **Rebuild the agency's pride, energy and self-belief.** Win a new client, one of which you can be really proud. New business wins have the ability to fire up an agency and raise its profile. A winning streak builds momentum and success attracts success on so many different levels. Develop some new campaigns for existing clients which build your pride due to their intrinsic content, the value generated, the profile raised and/or the results achieved. Think about how you can re-energise the agency's profile amongst its employees, clients and prospective clients.

Are you in the right state or are you in a right state?

Being in the right state is vital. The first sell is always to yourself. Before you can sell a proposal or a fee to a client, you must be totally convinced yourself of your ability and value. Occasionally, I meet account handlers who believe their agency fee levels are too high. This is a dangerous mindset if you want to sell your proposal credibly. If you are not convinced of the value of your proposal and expertise, then neither will your client be.

Stay on top of the marketplace. Make sure you are up to date with developments in your marketplace and that of your clients. Ensure you understand your clients, their industry and their customers. Don't live on past successes. There is no room for living on past glories.

3. **Really understand the true value you create for your client.** How clearly do you understand the value you create for your clients? Do your clients value your input sufficiently? I have seen agencies too focused on their 'implementation' and not taking the time to fully understand the value they provide. Once you know your value creation you can then more easily charge more realistic fees. By realistic I mean fees which are in relation to the value you have created or the output, rather than in relation to the input or hours taken to complete the task.

As well as you being clear about your agency's value, it is important to remind the client of your value and ensure you reinforce it. It is too easy for clients to take your value creation for granted.

Give existing clients the same effort you apply to new business pitches.

Clients want to know about the value you can create for them.

1. How MUCH value can you deliver?

2. How SOON can you deliver the value?

3. How LIKELY is it that you can deliver the value?

   Ideally, review your work with your clients every three to four months.

1. Remind the client of the original brief and background.

2. Ask how successful and valuable the agency's work has been. Really probe. Don't just accept the first answer.

3. Ask how the success can be measured and quantified.

4. **Monetise the value that you create for your clients.** Clearly assign hard and soft values to the results that you create for your clients. Monetise the pain that your client is experiencing and then provide a solution to take away that pain and therefore

deliver that corresponding value. This includes monetising IP, Intellectual Property.

It is vital to clarify this with the client. This will help your client obtain future budgets from their Finance Director and CEO who will be focused on Return on Investment and Payback. Some clients are reluctant to share this information too freely with their agency. Perhaps they are concerned the agency will want to be paid more when they realise the impact of their campaign for the client.

For example, if your client's brief is to generate 100,000 new customers, ask how much one customer is worth bottom line each year – say £10. Then ask how many years the average customer stays – say two years. Then, very simply, your campaign can generate:

100,000 (customers) x £10 (profit) x 2 years = £2m

Now position your fee in relation to the £2m generated rather than position your fee based on how many hours in your estimate it will take.

Alternatively, identify the cost of the problem to the client if nothing is done.

I have worked with US business and sales consultants who are totally focused on 'dollarising' the value they provide to their clients – much more so than UK consultants.

5. **Sell your expertise.** Charge what you are worth, not what you think your client will pay. Develop your expertise to be either unique or to be highly scarce. Is an hourly/daily rate the most appropriate way to be rewarded for the results you deliver for your clients? Or would value-based fees be a better and fairer form of remuneration? What is the expertise that you can develop? What is the expertise that your clients really value?

6. **Ensure you are 'sticky' – difficult to replace.** Find ways that make it difficult for the client to replace you. Perhaps based on your expertise, understanding of their business and customers. Perhaps your Intellectual Property in your ideas may help your stickiness.

7. **See your client as your peer.** Avoid simply implementing your client's requests. When appropriate, challenge their thinking, demonstrate your understanding and creative problem-solving. Speak with your client as an equal with specialist knowledge, and a mutual respect. This is an important point. It affects your mindset, thinking and, most importantly, your overall client-agency relationship. Do not tolerate unacceptable 'master-slave' behaviour from clients. Address this type of dysfunctional behaviour early. The reality is:

You get the behaviour you tolerate.

The longer you leave a difficult conversation, the harder it is and, conversely, the sooner you address a difficult conversation, the easier it is.

8. **Don't be too eager to please.** Even the name 'client service' suggests the wrong type of relationship between the agency and the client. There are too many reactive, passive and weak account management people in agencies. The priority of these reactive-passive account handlers seems to be simply delivery and doing their clients' bidding.

When I ask account handlers, "Who is too eager to please their clients?" at least two-thirds of the audience put their hands up. They look slightly embarrassed. They know it is not the right thing to do long term, but they do it for an easy life, so they think!

Their client likes it but rarely respects the individual or the agency. They come to expect it and want it even more and the relationship slips ever more towards 'buyer-supplier.' They then start seeing your work as 'implementation' and they realise it can be bought elsewhere as a commodity.

The best clients want an agency to add value, to challenge their thinking and to provide a competitive advantage. The best clients want that peer-to-peer, trusted adviser relationship where the agency applies its expertise to solve the client's challenges and problems. And yes, you can say 'no' to a client and retain your relationship; you will probably even improve it.

9. **Saying 'NO.'** The ability to say 'no' is one of the most powerful tools in negotiation. So let's see how we can use 'no' to help our negotiations.

The more <u>prepared</u> you are to say 'no' the more money you will make.

How many times each week do you say 'yes' to clients, colleagues and your boss when you should have said 'no?' Why do we seem to find it so hard to say 'no?'

Many of us have been conditioned to regard saying 'no' as impolite, unfriendly, uncooperative, even rude. We feel mean saying 'no.' We fear we may miss out on the deal.

There are some curious facts about the word 'no.' When you've said 'no' you can then subsequently say 'yes.' The reverse is not true. When you've said 'yes' it is very difficult to then say 'no.' Beware of saying 'yes' too readily.

So what actually happens when we say 'no?' Typically it creates surprise in the other party.

'No' changes the perception of power.

'No' demonstrates assertiveness.

'No' discourages further requests and 'nibbling.'

In some cases, the other party completely softens their position and becomes far more conciliatory.

So if you want to say 'no' but can't actually get the word out, there is a way to say 'no' without actually saying 'no!'

- "I can't hit your deadline of Friday, I need until the following Tuesday."

Giving options provides some sense of control to the other party and allows you to imply 'no.'

- "That's the price; which element shall we take out, A or B?"

- "Having this completed by Friday is impossible. I reckon Tuesday or Wednesday next week is more realistic."

- "If you want it for this Friday it will cost £3,000. If you give me till next Tuesday it will cost £2,500." (This is a great way to educate the client of the importance of giving you more time to complete work. Why is there a difference in price? To cover working through the night, hiring a freelancer, reallocating resource and other projects now to be worked on over the weekend etc.)

Knowing at what point you are prepared to say 'no' is vital in negotiations. Having a walk-away figure in your mind is so important when negotiating fees and prices. It doesn't need to be unfriendly, just said professionally. Just say:

"No, I can't do that, but I can do this."

10. **View your client's budget as an investment not a cost.** Encourage your client to see their budget also as an investment. Be clear about the return on investment they require. Increasingly, senior clients want a return on time as well as a specific ROI. Develop a robust business case to support your proposals, demonstrating the ROI, the payback, the pain avoided or reduced, or the gain achieved. The more clearly this is articulated, the better for both parties.

    See clients as investments. Invest more effort and time into those with the most likely payback and long-term profitability potential. Be selective where you invest your time. Learn the language of the C-suite (CEO, CFO, CMO, COO etc.) or boardroom. Move up the 'food-chain' and deal with senior decision-makers.

11. **Find points of distinctiveness that clients truly value.** Ask your clients what it is you do that they love; their answers will tell you a lot. I use the word 'love' deliberately. It is about understanding the emotional connection and the emotional needs that your agency fulfils. Collate the answers to this question that you receive from your different clients. What are you hearing across your client base that they love about your agency? Use the positive answers in your external communication with new clients. Your clients' words and phrases will resonate with new prospective clients. Listen carefully to their language. The greater your points of distinctiveness the better.

    Identify the rational and logical reasons that the client gives for why they choose to work with you. These points will be useful to know, especially in discussions with Procurement.

    Find a way to have precision focus on what your business is all about – what is it famous for in the eyes of its clients? What could it be famous for in the eyes of your ideal clients?

12. **Become a thought leader.** Develop your knowledge or a position on a particular topic so this becomes a powerful differentiator. Become the 'go to expert.' Rory Sutherland of Ogilvy Group in the UK has achieved this with his perspective, enthusiasm and knowledge of behavioural economics and how it can be used in advertising and marketing.

When the agency's mindset is on the front foot:

- The momentum of the agency builds in a more positive way

- The confidence leads to better and more innovative work

- The client-agency relationship improves and trust levels increase

- The dialogue between the two parties is more constructive

- You become 'employer of choice' and attract great talent

- There are fewer client complaints

- Both parties feel the remuneration and reward is fair for the value created

Rules of engagement

Right at the start of the client-agency relationship, agree the 'Best Practice for working together' – how you will work together in order to produce great work that delivers great results for your clients.

'Rules of engagement' for client-agency Best Practice for working together should be explained to clients in terms of the benefits they will enjoy: better, well thought through responses, better end results, more accuracy, better budget control, fewer mistakes and less re-works. This Best Practice should start from Day One, not three months after the appointment.

Tailor the Best Practice rules of engagement to your agency; however, rules should include:

- How briefs are given

- Budget guidelines

- Feedback to proposals and creative

- Communication

- Senior client contact

- Evaluation criteria

Develop client-agency rules of engagement relevant for your agency.

Face-to-face versus telephone versus email

The speed of change and technological developments mean we have more choices as to how to we communicate when we negotiate. Essentially, we have three main choices of communication when negotiating and each has its benefits and disadvantages. You need to consider which is the most appropriate and most effective in each case. 'Effective' is not necessarily the same as 'efficient.'

Face-to-face: People win business, paper doesn't. Generally face-to-face is preferable and more effective for negotiations than the telephone or email. Next time you are about to email or post your proposal to a client, stop. Book a time to take the client through the proposal face-to-face. That way you can see and hear their feedback and reactions. You can probably handle there and then any concerns or objections. There will also be opportunities to build rapport, relationships and ultimately, trust.

Take time to prepare for your face-to-face negotiations. When discussing the price or quotation, you can more easily assess their position. By watching their body language you can pick up on various clues. I have certainly found clients are less aggressive in negotiations face-to-face than on the phone or by email. It is essential afterwards to confirm in writing key decisions and negotiations agreed during a meeting.

Telephone: The telephone is brilliant in terms of speed and accessibility. However, there are three inherent dangers with the phone.

First, we can't see the other party's reactions and body language during our conversation and negotiation. It is therefore much harder to judge their response.

Secondly, many people don't feel the need to plan and prepare for negotiations on the telephone in the same way we might prepare for a face-to-face negotiation meeting. It is therefore easy to find yourself 'shooting from the hip' and agreeing to something which you later regret when you put the phone down.

Thirdly, things happen very quickly on the phone, much quicker generally than in a face-to-face situation. This exacerbates the lack of preparation.

In addition, pauses and silences can be very powerful or disconcerting on the phone, depending on whether you have gone silent or you are experiencing silence from the other party.

As with meetings, it is essential to confirm in writing key decisions and negotiations agreed during a telephone call.

Email: Email is fast and efficient. However, it can be dangerous in the context of negotiations. The danger is that when you email a proposal to a client complete with costings and fees, the typical reaction of most clients is to turn immediately to the costings, and if it is within their limits they then might read the rest of the proposal – or should that be 'skim-read' or should that be 'put to the side to read later?' (Our agency used to have a client who, in meetings, would grab the proposal document from my hand and always turn to the costings page at the back. In the end, I smartened up and kept the costings in a separate document. You can take the same approach with email).

Clients can easily be much more aggressive by email which makes it very difficult to understand their wider concerns, what they liked in the proposal and their overall reaction. Now you are on the back-foot with your costings being challenged and beaten down.

Some major corporates now email their brief to the agency and want the creative approach, proposal and costings emailed back to them. I am sure this saves time; however, I am concerned for the quality of the relationship between the client and agency, the motivation of the agency team and increasing commoditisation of agencies. It is hard to be a trusted adviser without some quality face-to-face contact.

If your client is a great distance from the agency, such as in another country, I can understand the need to use email for proposals, creative work and budgets so prolifically.

I recommend a 'blended' communication approach to negotiations whereby face-to-face and telephone are used initially to build rapport and the relationship. Then use email to confirm the details of the negotiation agreed.

So by using the right principles of negotiation and being in the right mindset, we can now think about how we can work more effectively with our clients. Enjoy the next chapter: 'Work Smarter, Not Harder.'

CHAPTER 4

Work smarter, not harder

Key points in this chapter

Think more and run less to improve the effectiveness of your work

- Generate profitable income

- Profit is not simply the difference between your revenue and overheads

- A wide range of influences can impact your profitability

Do you tolerate unprofitable clients?

How much are unprofitable clients costing you?

In the 1980s, BT ran a major TV campaign called 'work smarter, not harder' to demonstrate the efficiency benefits of the telephone. This phrase is highly relevant today with reference to the benefits which accrue to agencies from effective negotiations.

When you negotiate more effectively, you will work smarter by increasing your long-term remuneration whilst not working any harder.

The $64,000 question - So how can we make more money, build better relationships with our clients, increase our client-agency security and work fewer hours?

1. Stop running, think, plan and act

I see many of my clients working in agencies running faster and faster just to stand still. It is a classic dilemma they are facing. As financial targets are increased or seem harder to achieve, so the tendency is to think the only answer is simply to run faster.

I am convinced that paradoxically the exact opposite is required.

Take time to stop, think and plan your work more.

Running my own business, I can see now so clearly the importance of finding time to THINK. If I don't take time to think about my business, my clients and the value I provide, then who will?

Similarly, within agencies if the senior agency team are not taking regular time to think and plan the business, consider the agency's profitability and to think about their clients' business, then the agency is like a sailing boat at the mercy of the wind and tides. It may feel like progress but is it in the direction you want to go?

Churchill said:

"We have no money, we shall have to think."

When we have less money and budgets are tight, we need to think more clearly, more creatively and more innovatively.

2. Work <u>on</u> the business, not <u>in</u> the business

In many agencies, the owners and senior directors work closely in the business running and managing core client business, which is why many clients hire the agency in the first place. The dilemma is that it is great for clients having senior people working on their business; however, the danger is that because they are so immersed in the day-to-day implementation of client projects, they leave too little time to think about the development and direction of the agency and its people.

Gandhi once said:

'I used to meditate for 2 hours every day.
As I have got busier so I meditate for 4 hours every day.'

Replace the word 'meditate' with the word 'plan.'

'I used to plan for 2 hours every day.
As I have got busier so I plan for 4 hours every day.'

How much time is enough time to plan the development and success of the agency? It will vary from business to business. As a rough rule of thumb, for senior agency management I would suggest an absolute minimum of ½ day/week – that's only 10 % of the time, ideally it should be substantially more. In addition, every month and every quarter take an extra full day to work on the business. This equates to less than 20 % of your working time. Does that seem a big investment to ensure your agency is on track to grow and develop?

3. Focus on your value to your clients

Value as a word seems to have several different definitions, some of which contradict each other. 'Value supermarkets' in the UK, the likes of Aldi and Lidl, have hijacked the definition of value to mean 'cheap.' That is not the 'value' I am referring to!

When I use the term 'value' I define it as what is valuable to the client. Value, like beauty, is in the eye of the beholder. It is personal, specific and not always obvious.

It is how your client is better off after your intervention. What results does the client enjoy after your activity?

Typically our clients want results and certainty such as increased sales, improved distribution, increased customer penetration, increased display, increased market share/market position, risk reduction and so on. Some of these are hard, tangible measures and others are softer, intangible measures. It is vital to understand what it is that your client values and wants to buy.

I heard an interesting definition for value:

*Value is a mystery.**

The more I reflected on this, the more appropriate the definition became. What is value to our clients is a mystery until we ask them, using the right questions. Value to our clients is not what we assume it is.

However, typically what we sell to clients is 'what we do' – i.e. direct marketing, advertising, PR, design, digital – I'm sure you get the picture.

Stop selling, and help your client buy.

Let me illustrate this with a poignant example. I was working with a major client who sells recruitment advertising to a variety of industries. How I summed up the approach of 'stop selling and help your client to buy' to their sales force was:

Stop selling recruitment advertising and help your client find the right candidate.

* Thanks to Mike Wilkinson for this definition

Typically, advertising sales people are focused on selling advertising space in their publication rather than helping their clients achieve their specific outcomes. When we focus too much on our outcomes it can often be to the detriment of our client's outcome.

You have now put yourself in the shoes of your client and are seeing the opportunity from their perspective (of finding the right candidate), not your perspective (of selling the advertising space or hitting your sales target).

Great negotiators have the ability to take time to see the issue, deal or negotiation from the other party's perspective. When you do this it changes your thinking, your words and, most importantly, the response you get from your client. Step into your client's shoes and see the deal from their perspective.

How do we find out what our clients really value? By asking them great questions to understand their perspective.

Some years ago I was developing a major advertising and direct marketing campaign for an important client who had allocated £1.5m budget whilst requiring a large increase in sales. We had a legal issue to resolve. I contacted our company legal advisers who told me the issue was too complex for them to solve. I needed a QC (Queen's Counsel barrister – one of the most experienced and senior lawyers). They recommended one specific QC, John, who specialised in this particular legal area. Our legal advisers told me that if anyone could give me an answer, John could, but he was 'very expensive.' If my memory serves me correctly, he charged £600/hour and this was around 1990. Somewhat in shock, I decided that I still needed this crucial advice so agreed to visit John in Lincoln's Inn, London – the home of many leading lawyers with very high hourly rates.

John greeted me by asking, "So you think £600/hour is a lot of money? Let me explain what you get for £600. Yes, you get an hour of my time, but more importantly you get the 30 years of my experience to give you the right answer." Suddenly the £600 seemed good value. My mistake was to focus on his hourly rate, not the value of his advice to me.

Ever since that day I have appreciated the difference between price and value. Hourly rates simply commoditise your expertise. Pay me for the results I deliver, not for simply showing up. Think about how your client is better off – the outcome or the result. Understand what that value is and how it can be quantified. Can you use this to position your agency fee? Unfortunately, the hourly and daily rate method of charging is so pervasive for agencies it is difficult to avoid.

PAIN–GAIN

Freud identified that we are psychologically motivated to move away from pain and to move towards pleasure. This principle applies in selling.

Clients are typically motivated to move away from PAIN and move towards GAIN.

In most cases, PAIN is substantially more powerful as a motivator psychologically than GAIN. Find out about your client's PAIN. Understand their challenges that they need to overcome. Do this by asking great questions. If the PAIN is great enough, clients will always find the budget to make the PAIN go away or reduce. Monetise your client's PAIN and then find an appropriate solution.

Do you really know what your client values? Or do you assume you know what they value? Or did you know a few years ago and haven't updated your knowledge by assuming nothing has changed? Most businesses are changing so fast it is important to check at least on an annual basis how things are changing. Everything is changing and if it hasn't, it's about to. It is so easy after a few years working with a client to assume you know what they value, what their pain is and what gain they want to achieve.

GIGO

The client's brief is the fundamental starting point for an agency working with a client. Often the quality of the client's brief is not as good as it should be, yet it will influence the agency's output considerably.

'Garbage In, Garbage Out.' The quality of the brief that you receive from your clients is crucial in your ability to develop great solutions to help your client overcome their challenges and move away from their PAIN.

The right brief will help the agency to understand the value to the client and provide clarity in the direction required.

Three essential ingredients that every great brief must have are:

OBJECTIVE: what is the objective to be achieved?

SUCCESS: how will you judge the success? What will success look like? What will be really valuable to you?

MEASUREMENT: how will you measure this success? What metrics will you use to evaluate the success?

The last two areas, success and measurement, may seem obvious but are often omitted by the client and agency from the brief.

You then need time and confidence to think through your client's brief. You need inspired fresh thinking. You need to think strategically, tactically and creatively. Great briefs give you clarity, focus your thinking and also make evaluation afterwards much easier and more relevant.

1. Focus on the profitability of your clients to your business

Draw a standard distribution curve comparing number of clients with levels of profitability to the agency. Identify the three different clusters of clients.

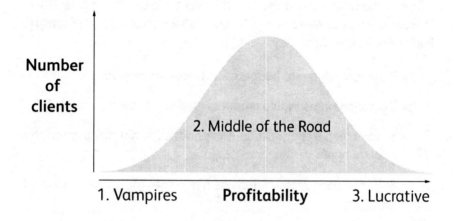

Then develop strategies for each of the three clusters of clients in order to improve the agency's profitability levels.

1. Profit Vampires: Perversely, as well as draining your profits these are often clients who are the most costly to service. In some cases it actually costs the agency money to service these clients. Why are they tolerated? Is it because they are a big, well-known brand name? Is it because they are a long-standing client 'protected' by one senior agency member who tells everyone 'you don't understand client xyz?'

Or they are 'trophy clients' the agency has had for years whose fees have not been increased for years, yet the scope and type of work has increased and changed.

How many trophy clients can an agency afford?

Trophy clients are unprofitable clients who are on the client list and tolerated for reasons of profile, prestige and even simply inertia.

Ironically it also seems that the profit vampires are the most loyal clients to the agency. (I wonder if that's because they know that no other agency would tolerate their low level of profitability).

Identify the critical reason(s) why the client is a profit vampire. Often there is a range of reasons which cumulatively drain your profitability. For example, the client may:

- Provide inadequate budgets for the results required

- Demand unreasonable amounts of senior time unnecessarily

- Scope creep the project so it expands substantially beyond the original brief

- Bully the agency team and use fear to get more than they paid for

Once the reason(s) is/are identified you can then decide how each problem can be tackled.

I recommend that your strategy with the profit vampires is that you 'ship 'em up or ship 'em out' – raise your fee and rates and/or reduce the team overhead cost by reducing your hours, or reduce the seniority of some team members. The argument against this is that the client generates turnover. I can appreciate this benefit, but only in the short term; long term, the situation needs to be resolved. Sometimes it seems that turnover is used as an excuse to avoid resolving the situation. The freed-up resource can now work on more lucrative clients or business development (if you are losing money on this type of client, almost anything else is a better use of time). Or simply part company with the vampire clients, but one at a time.

Don't tackle your profit vampires all at the same time. Take a planned approach. Start with the worst profit vampire, i.e. the least profitable client. Ideally, resolve that situation, then learn from the process and move on to the next profit vampire. Convert them into profitable clients, one at a time. Don't expect overnight miracles but at least start the profitability improvement journey.

If a profit vampire won't agree to the increased rates or change of fee, maybe it's time to pass them to your competitor!

I appreciate this is not an easy decision. If you want to improve your agency's profitability you have either got to let go of your profit vampires or resolve the situation by converting them into more profitable clients.

(They say one of the first signs of madness is doing nothing different and expecting a different result).

If you are really serious about improving your agency's profitability, then every one or two years consider firing your bottom 5-10% of clients, especially those who won't agree to any increases in fees or rates, whilst replacing them with more profitable clients. There is no point in growing an agency infested with unprofitable clients.

This is easier said than done; however, it should be a key part of the agency's business development strategy to attract more profitable clients.

Diagnosis	Action
Fee levels and day-rates too low	Monetise the value that you've created and forecast. Compare your rates to market rates. Discuss a small increase in fee with the client, based on results delivered and value provided. Consider PBR (Payment By Results).
Substantial amount of work being done for free. Variety of possible reasons:	Log and quantify the amount of work done for free or low cost. Monetise the value of that work. Discuss with the client and resolve.
1. Client scope creeping.	Explain to the client this work is outside the scope of the agreement and therefore you must charge accordingly.
2. Scope seep	This is when the agency willingly provides extra work without the client asking for it. The agency over-services, assuming this will keep the client happy long term. Generally this is a false and mistaken strategy. Educate the account team.
3. Weak client management	Educate the account person and work with them to be more assertive and to understand the value they deliver to their clients.
4. Changes and re-work costs not being fully recovered.	Log, measure and quantify. Understand the reasons why. Explain to the client these changes need to be charged for. Set up systems and processes to reduce changes and re-works in future.
Highly competitive roster of agencies keeping prices and rates depressed.	Assess importance of client to agency and what the client values that you provide. What does the client see as your agency's key strengths and differentiators? Act according to the importance of this client to the agency. Make some changes if you want an improvement in profitability.
New clients being won at below normal day-rates.	This can be caused by a sense of desperation, lack of confidence or lack of understanding in the value provided or the agency has become commoditised. This cannot continue. All new fee proposals to be approved by a senior individual.

Review and diagnose each client to identify the key reasons which are holding back increasing the potential profitability and then select the top three actions that will make an improvement to that client's contribution to the agency's profitability.

2. Middle of the Road clients

This is where the majority of your clients are likely to be. Look for opportunities to increase the profitability of these middle of the road clients. Find ways to increase your fee rates, even by only 1-2% each year. Identify areas where you may be missing out on additional profitability, such as scope creep.

Seek continuous profitability improvement from the account teams.

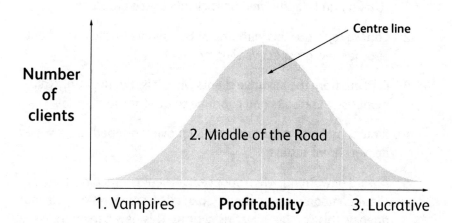

Draw a vertical line in the middle of the standard distribution curve through the middle of the road clients. Then, whenever you win a new client or project to the left of the vertical line, that new client or new project will be pulling down the rest of the business. Whenever you win a new client or project to the right of the vertical line, it will be moving the business towards a more profitable position.

What does this mean to an agency? It is like running on a treadmill and changing the incline. To the left of the centre line with a steeper incline you will run faster simply to stand still. This is not a long-term profitable strategy. To the right of the centre line the incline reduces and profitability improves.

It's not good enough to win business, you have to win profitable business from both existing and new clients.

3. Lucrative/high reward clients

Most agencies that I have worked with have a relatively small number of highly profitable clients. What should be the negotiation strategy with these clients?

1. Understand clearly why these clients are so profitable.

2. Can we replicate this with any of our middle of the road clients or other new prospective clients?

3. Find out from the lucrative clients what it is that they truly value, monetise the results and continue to delight the client(s).

4. Protect and retain these clients by providing superb work which delivers great results.

5. A word of warning: when your senior client contact in a lucrative client company leaves and is replaced by someone new to your agency, this can be a very risky time. This new person may see your fee levels and charges as much higher than they have experienced from the agencies used at their previous company. They may therefore run a competitive pitch or demand a reduction in fees.

6. Ensure you have excellent relationships at the most senior level in the client company with the real decision-makers.

A few years ago I worked with a B2B financial services company with the brief to improve their overall profitability. We analysed their whole client base against revenue. Unfortunately, they were unable to analyse profitability by individual client, only revenue by individual client. The profitability would have been even more pronounced than the revenue by client. The findings into how the revenue split by decile of clients makes interesting reading. They had around 600 clients.

Their top 10% of clients (60) accounted for 30% of their revenue.

Their top 20% of clients (120) accounted for 53% of their revenue.

Just 16 clients generated their top 10% of revenue (that's less than 3% of their client base).

219 clients generated their bottom 10% of revenue (that's 36% of their client base).

Where would you allocate your time and resources with a client base like that?

What would be your strategy with the bottom 10% of clients (60), which accounted for around 1% of their revenue?

Pareto's Rule is an interesting benchmark to consider at this point. Typically, 20% of clients will account for around 80% of a business's profits. It is not an exact figure but it is often reasonably close. Not all clients are equal and the danger is that the typical long tail of clients can be unprofitable.

Vilfredo Pareto was an Italian economist who observed that 80% of the land in Italy was owned by 20% of the population. He then observed how this relationship was common in many other situations – that a small proportion can produce the majority of results. It is not a hard and fast rule but is definitely a useful indicator or rule of thumb. For example, typically:

- 20 % of the sales force will produce 80 % of the sales

- 80 % of complaints come from 20 % of your customer base

- We wear 20 % of our clothes 80 % of the time

It's about understanding where the leverage is. Within your business, what are the few things you and your people can do to have a huge impact on achieving your business goals?

How else can we evaluate the profitability of a client?

There are a variety of criteria to evaluate the profitability of a client over and above their pure revenue and direct profit contribution. Some of these criteria are subjective and will vary from agency to agency depending on the circumstances. These are in no particular order:

- **Cash flow:** What are their payment terms? How readily do they pay? How much time do you spend chasing payment? If a client takes nine months or more to pay, your cash flow is depleted; also so much time is wasted chasing their accounts department for payment.

- **Regularity of work:** Is there a steady stream of work keeping the team well occupied or are there seasonal changes, pronounced peaks and troughs in the work-loads? Resource allocation is becoming an increasingly important factor as agencies try to squeeze every drop of optimised resource they can from their people.

- **Last-minute or planned:** Is the client's work steady and does it have appropriate lead times or is it all consistently left to the last minute by the client? Last-minute and late work can be very expensive to service for any agency. Generally, the most profitable work is a consistent, steady stream allowing careful planning of workloads and resource allocation. Some agencies also tell me that quick turnaround, highly-intensive projects can be very profitable short term. I would recommend you charge a premium price for last-minute projects to cover disruption, reallocation of resource, possible freelance resource and to educate the client to brief with adequate lead times where possible. I do not accept that everything has to be done in a rush.

You do your best work when you have time to think.

When you do work in a rush, there is an increased likelihood that it will not be so well thought through, mistakes are more likely to arise and it may even be less effective. Clients remember those mistakes long after they have forgotten how quickly you completed the project. Clients don't really appreciate rushed work although they think they do! Clients appreciate great work that delivers or exceeds the results they need.

- **Changes and 'hassle' factor:** Change and hassle can affect the profitability of a client to an agency. Re-works are expensive. Multiple re-works are highly expensive and can also affect the relationship negatively. How much aggravation does a client create for an agency when they make multiple sets of amends?

- **Scope-creep:** Does this client regularly scope creep us? This is a huge problem for many agencies.

- **Credibility and profile:** Does this client raise the agency's profile and credibility? Does this client attract other new clients and enable us to 'punch above our weight?' Does this client raise our credibility in a specific industry that's important for our development? (Profile may come at a high price! One agency advised me that their client, a major fmcg company, wanted to charge the agency for displaying the client's logo in the agency's reception. Another, a major spirits company, assessed the value of their name on the agency's client list as worth thousands of pounds per year to be deducted from the agency's fees).

- **Referrals and introductions:** Does this client introduce us and refer us to other clients within their company, group or other external companies? Referrals and introductions can be a very valuable and useful source of new business. I have worked with several agencies to help them to develop their referral strategy which has become a highly-effective new business generation tool.

Prioritisation

Whether we are Martin Sorrell or the most junior account executive in an agency, we all have 24 hours in a day – not a second more or a second less. How we choose to spend that time will have a huge impact on our productivity and profitability.

In the mid 1990s I was introduced to Dr. Stephen Covey's quadrants assessing 'importance and urgency.' This made me think more carefully about how I allocated my time to various tasks. This is a simple four-box matrix.

	Urgent	Not urgent
Important	Quadrant I: Crisis, pressing problems, firefighting, deadlines, emails, phone calls, some meetings	Quadrant II: Preparation, fire prevention, planning, relationship-building, appraisals, some meetings
Not important	Quadrant III Interruptions, some mail, some emails, some phone calls, some meetings	Quadrant IV Trivia, time-wasters, escape activity, excessive TV

Typically we spend too much time in Quadrant I and not enough time in Quadrant II. When you spend just a little more time in Quadrant II it actually makes it easier to cope with the challenges of Quadrant I. There are different profit opportunities associated with Quadrants I and II. Quadrant I is often about immediate revenue, today's money and can be very 'seductive' of our time and focus. Quadrant II is often about the planning and generation of future longer-term revenue. It tends to be strategic and harder for many of us who find it easier to remain in our comfort zone, implementing. There is a danger that Quadrant II is ignored and reasons are found to put those activities off until another day. It is easy to be too focused on the immediate short term.

You may have noticed I haven't mentioned Quadrants III & IV – I don't want to spend any time on them!

The nicest thing about not planning is that failure comes as a complete surprise and is not preceded by a period of worry and depression.

John Preston, Boston College

I sometimes hear account handling delegates on workshops telling me that 'it's not their fault.' The nature and culture of their client is all last-minute. I can appreciate that some clients' businesses are like this. However, take responsibility and help your client to plan better and then they, and you, will be able to cope with real last-minute crises and panics more effectively. The other benefit will be to spend their budgets more wisely. A client is more likely to stay longer with an agency when you have helped them develop and improve their work processes as well as delivered enormous monetised value.

How well is your agency differentiated from your competitors? The more differentiated, and in ways that your clients value, the more effectively you will be able to negotiate more profitably. The next chapter will help you consider your agency's differentiation and also your agency's approach to winning new clients.

CHAPTER 5

Differentiation and winning business

Key points

- The importance of differentiating your agency

- How to differentiate your agency

- How differentiation can give you the potential to charge a premium price, be more profitable and improve your ability to negotiate

The danger of chasing after increasingly smaller opportunities.

Are you chasing anything with a budget?

Commoditisation is increasingly common in many industries as competitors converge and appear to be similar; their points of difference become marginal. As commoditisation happens, so price quickly becomes the key determinant for the client. If you appear to be the same as your competitors, why should a client pay a premium price for what is essentially the same thing? If you want to make more money by charging a premium price then you need to be really clear why a client should pay more.

Procurement will deliberately exacerbate the commoditisation of your business; for example, by developing a simple pricing matrix to compare your prices with those of your competitors. Procurement will generally see price as a crucial deciding factor.

The more you can differentiate your company and your services in ways that your client values, the easier it will be for you to be able to attract the client to choose you and for you to justify charging a premium price.

> *The riskiest thing is to play safe and conversely*
> *the safest thing is to be risky.*
> Seth Godin

Taking what appears to be the safe route can often be the least safe choice because the safe route can be bland and lack standout from the crowd. Taking the riskier route can be a better choice by providing a difference and standout from your competitors. So what gives us standout?

Factors to differentiate your agency

These factors should be considered when planning how to differentiate your agency.

Features, advantages, benefits, value

Features are things that a product or service has, does or offers. For example, saying to a new prospective client, 'Our agency has experience of your industry sector.'

Advantages are the clever implications of that feature. So in the example above, with a new prospective client, 'Our experience makes the agency better able to understand the issues and challenges of your industry.'

Benefits mean something to your customer on a personal level and so can be difficult to guess accurately, so they may have to be uncovered. In our example, 'Our experience of your sector means the agency is more likely to find a great solution more quickly making you, the client, more money, saving you money and time with less likelihood of mistakes and errors.'

Value is how the benefits tie into what's important to the customer. Each of us defines them in our own terms. When you offer true value your customer will 'happily' pay a higher price for your product or service. For example, a senior client may see value in your agency's experience to save them time so they can focus on developing a new product which will raise their profile in the company and in the eyes of their global CEO.

Features alone are generally not persuasive reasons to buy and are often commoditised in the mind of the client. Many sales people will typically spray their client with generic features until they see a sign they've possibly said something of interest. Most people don't buy features. People buy benefits and values – specifically the benefits and values which are important to them. When you sell these specific benefits and values as opposed to generic features, your sales conversion rate will increase dramatically.

To convert a feature into a benefit, add the phrase

'**.....which means that....**'

If you can say 'So what?' then it's not a benefit – or certainly not a persuasive and uncommoditised benefit.

Feature		Benefit
Air-conditioned car	*Which means that*	You are cool and comfortable

Agencies often use generic features to describe the agency such as 'database specialist,' 'biggest agency in...' or 'highly creative.' Translate your agency's features into the benefits to the client.

In the left column are some typical examples of features that agencies use to describe themselves to clients. In the right column the features have been converted into benefits to the client.

Typical Agency Feature	(which means that) Benefit to the Client
Database specialists	We can help you find your most and least profitable customers so you can spend your marketing budget more efficiently.
Biggest agency in our sector	We have more experience and are more likely to find the right solution to solve your problems. Our tried and tested processes will ensure your budgets are invested most effectively.
Highly creative	We can help you stand out in a crowded marketplace. We can engage and connect with your niche audience better than your competitors. More importantly, we can get that audience to take action.

Taking a more consultative approach

You must take a consultative approach and become a trusted adviser to your client or prospect.

Taking a more consultative approach improves your ability to negotiate effectively with your clients. Think about how you can be more consultative with your clients.

What are the factors which increase your consultative ability?

- **Questioning ability:** The quality and crafting of your questions will demonstrate your expertise and therefore your distinctiveness from other agencies.

- **Listening ability:** Listening skills are easily overlooked and yet are vital. When asked what frustrates clients about 'professional services people', typically the top two frustrations are 'they don't understand my business' and 'they don't listen.' Don't just listen to what is being said; listen to how it's said and listen to what's not said. Active listening is needed to encourage the other party to give up and share more and more information.

- **Understanding your client's business/industry:** Ensure a sound grasp of the factors and the key trends affecting the client's industry. This is a prerequisite that clients look for in an agency. What do you need to do in order to understand your client's customers better than they do?

- **Ability to influence:** Be able to lead and provide a persuasive argument. Develop your influencing skills and improve what you say and how you say it.

- **Business acumen:** Develop a sound grasp of business principles and the factors affecting business over and above the marketing communication issues. Develop your broad business understanding. Be curious. Read the financial press, business books and attend relevant conferences and seminars to provide some fresh perspective. This is also useful in developing credibility with senior level clients.

- **Subject matter expertise:** Clients want specialists. Specialists reduce the client's risk and increase their certainty of success. Generalists can be viewed as commodities and lacking value. Consider how you can develop your expertise in ways your clients value.

- **Ability to think laterally and effectively:** Develop your critical thinking skills and ability to think strategically and clearly. Clients typically pay a premium for quality thinking in favour of implementation.

- **Ability to see the big picture:** It is important to see the wider context and the broader implications for the client's business. As you become more senior it is vital to lift yourself out of the detail. Detail is like quicksand – it pulls you down and it is imperative to rise actively above it. Most senior decision-makers have a big picture approach. Listen to their words and language – speak their 'language' back to them.

- **Ability to find insights and patterns within data:** Great consultants are able to sift through a mass of data and information and pick out the most important trends and learnings. Identify trends the client hasn't yet seen. See the data from a new perspective.

- **Speaks the language of business:** In other words, talk about investment, return, payback, profit....Talk the language of the boardroom or C-suite (CEO, COO, CFO, CMO etc).

Why should I do business with your company?

Imagine you are in conversation with the Marketing Director of your ideal prospective client and you are asked this question. How convincingly are you able to answer this question?

If you were the prospective client, would it persuade you to continue the conversation and to want to know more? This is such as easy question to ask but often so difficult to answer for many companies. How consistent and compelling would the answer be from your colleagues across the agency to this question?

Most companies have such an unconvincing answer to the question *'why should I do business with your company?'*

As you consider how best to respond to this question, reflect on the following:

- Avoid truisms, clichés and platitudes such as: 'We are really creative, we're results-focused and we're really passionate' – points that clients will have heard a hundred times before from your competitors.

- Clients aren't interested in what you sell. They are interested in the results you deliver – how they will be better off after your intervention.

'30-second elevator speech'

Although the concept of the 30-second elevator speech was developed some years ago in the US, it is still a useful discipline to work on in order to clarify what your proposition should be – for you and your company. It should be created by involving a number of the agency team to ensure ownership of the words.

Imagine you are travelling in an elevator (lift) at a business conference with another conference delegate. In the lift you are both wearing your conference name badges. You notice the other delegate's badge and realise they would be an ideal client for your agency. This senior prospective client turns to you, looks at your badge and asks, "So what does ABC agency do?" Is your answer compelling enough so that the prospect turns to you to say, "Have you got a business card? Give me a call, we should talk further."

Or is your answer so mundane and uninspiring that the prospect isn't interested in talking further to you? If your answer is simply along the lines of "We're an ad agency" or "We're a digital agency" then you need to think again.

Take time to craft your 30-second elevator speech. It should be a short, compelling description of what you do, who you do it for and how they benefit. It should have a natural flow – perhaps no more than 10-20 words. I also believe it is sensible to tailor it to your audience and to have several for use in different situations, talking to clients in different industries and with different requirements.

Take time to develop several 30-second elevator speeches. They should flow naturally, be compelling and authentic. They will vary according to the prospect's company, situation and their title/role.

There is no one right answer. It is good to have a small selection which the members of the agency like and are comfortable with so there is a consistent message from everyone. The acid test is whether it provokes the start of a useful new business conversation. If not, craft it until you develop one that does.

<u>Tips to make your 30-second elevator speech more compelling</u>

- Humour can be useful within your 'speech' especially if it resonates well with the audience and their challenges

- The more specific the content the better

- For extra credibility give examples of the companies you work with

- Provocative can be persuasive

- Topical can be interesting

- If you can, include figures, e.g. '25 % increase' 'four-fold increase in...' to give more appeal

- Whatever you do, make sure it sounds different from your competitors

Stories create distinctiveness

Short memorable business stories are a powerful way to differentiate your agency from competitors and create an emotional connection. Short memorable stories go further than the 30-second elevator speech. The short story can be used after the 30-second elevator speech to elaborate and when the prospect has said, 'tell me more.'

It's said that **facts tell, stories sell.**

Story-telling is a powerful communication between people and the majority of people are intrigued by interesting and compelling stories. Don't tell your story too early. Make sure you know what topics or hot buttons are important to the prospective client first.

Develop a selection of interesting stories (say six) for your agency, each story addressing a different aspect of your business, experience or expertise. These stories need to have a natural flow. They need to be emotive and enticing, not a boring case-study. The use of the 'list of three' is powerful (our brains like threes).

Selectivity

The more prepared you are to say 'no' the more money you will make.

How does this paradox work? When you are desperate for business, you give away clues to the client in your body language, your verbal language and your demeanour, whereas when you see yourself as equal to your client, peer to peer, you will come across as more confident in the value that you deliver to clients.

Of course, I'm not suggesting arrogance. I simply recommend that when you take pride, and believe in the value you provide, your level of confidence and self-belief will increase.

It seems that the most successful agencies take care to select the right clients and new business prospects for their business. Like any relationship, it is a two-way process. Choose your clients carefully.

- Choose clients that see you as a peer with expertise to help solve their problems

- Choose clients whose culture brings out the best in you and your work

- Choose clients who value your contribution to their business

- Choose clients who are prepared to reward you fairly and in line with the contribution you make to their business

- Avoid clients who see the agency solely as a resource for implementation

- Develop a list of criteria to help you screen and select prospective new clients

- Avoid clients who do not match your selection criteria reasonably closely

  Is this easy to do? It will mean tough choices for you. The choices are even tougher when you really need the business because your business isn't performing well. Survival often means making some tough choices.

- Decide what your long-term goal is for your agency; for example, to have:

- A strong robust business with sustainable revenues

- A broad selection of great clients

- Clients who value your contribution

- Clients who are prepared to reward you properly

Why do agencies win new clients?

Whenever I ask this question in a workshop, I generally get similar answers which include words like chemistry, strategic thinking, fresh thinking, great ideas, energy, reputation, contacts, prepared to challenge and occasionally, costs. Fees and remuneration are subsequently agreed on the promise of delivering more of the same.

The trap to avoid after the initial honeymoon phase is that the agency moves into the 'implementation' phase and the focus is primarily on 'delivery.' Implementation then dominates and the agency becomes like a sausage machine. What has happened to the strategic thinking, the fresh thinking, the great ideas, the energy and the preparedness to challenge? The challenge, fresh thinking and new ideas from the early days of the relationship become a distant memory. In some cases, they get channelled into that next new business pitch to a different client. Implementation, or the sausage machine, continues until someone at the client company questions the agency's contribution and the value provided. Quite often this happens when the main client has a new boss or, worse, your main client leaves and the agency is now working with the successor who sees the incumbent agency's work as tame, tactical and predictable. By now it is probably too late to upgrade your service from sausage machine back to the original innovative standard demonstrated in the pitch at the start of the relationship.

How can we avoid this dilemma?

- Ensure you have regular strategic conversations with the senior decision-makers in your client's company. Find out what their top three to five critical issues are. Keep those critical issues front of mind for the team.

- Continue to provide new solutions to the client's new and ongoing problems. Better still, find solutions to problems they haven't yet discovered.

- Perhaps have a senior colleague on another client account

review your work with you to identify new opportunities via their different and 'naïve' perspective. Do the same for them on a quid pro quo basis.

- View the client not as an existing client but a prospective one. Give them the energy and effort you put into your new business pitches.

- Find subtle ways to demonstrate your value. Have conversations in which the client tells you about the value you've created for their business.

- Turn up your 'antennae' to pick up any clues that the client may not be 100% happy with your service:

  - Do they return calls as readily?

  - Do they seem as friendly and forthcoming with information and when asked questions?

  - Do they discuss long-term plans as readily?

Why do agencies lose clients?

Why does any relationship come to an end? Because one or both parties are no longer feeling as satisfied by the value they are deriving and often then feel they can do better elsewhere.

From my observations and discussions with clients and agencies it seems that, initially, small cracks of dissatisfaction appear in the relationship. Early on they don't seem important enough to resolve. The agency is probably aware something is wrong but not totally sure what is actually wrong. The agency assumes the problem will go away or that they are imagining things. At this early stage, the issues are often still resolvable. It takes effort to tease them out in conversation. Most of us avoid confrontation – that's both the agency and the client.

So we don't find out about the cracks early on. Time passes, the cracks grow a little more. Something happens on the account – a minor problem, perhaps, that in the past would have been accepted and now is seen by the client as really frustrating. Now there is a danger of going past the 'point of no return.' The client withdraws slightly. There are subtle changes in the relationship. Phone calls are not returned by the client. Conversations between the agency and client are less relaxed. Information from the client is less forthcoming. Discussions about future plans when raised by the agency are avoided.

Do not wait for your client-agency relationship to get to this stage. Ensure your finger is on the pulse of the client-agency relationship. Find ways to spot the early signs, those minor cracks in the relationship and reduction in trust levels. Trust your instincts.

Ensure you have regular opportunities (minimum quarterly) to touch base and have a frank and open conversation with the senior decision-maker(s) at the client company. Plan your questions and watch their body language for signs of hesitation.

Have an independent researcher visit your key clients to question them on your service. I have seen this done many times and it seems that clients are often more forthcoming to a stranger than to the agency directly.

From a recent study of client-agency relationships by the AAR (Advertising Agency Register), clients have become substantially less tolerant in the first few months from appointment. A newly-appointed agency has very little time to impress their new client – perhaps a month or two at most. The duration of their tolerance has halved in three years.

Easy question to ask, tough question to answer

One of my favourite questions to ask my agency clients is:

> *'If you lost your most important client tomorrow what would be the most likely reason?'*

Whatever the answer, the next thing simply to say is, 'then sort it out.'

Our next challenge is deciding how much to charge clients for our work. How do we decide what level the fee should be? How do we ensure our fee is profitable? Turn to the next chapter.

CHAPTER 6

Pricing profitably

Key learnings

- The black art and science of pricing

- How best to position our price

- The dangers of discounting and dropping our price

- How to handle price challenges

Do you think clients decide solely on price?

I have no silver bullet solutions and no quick fixes. For many companies, pricing is the worst-managed area of marketing. Mark Ritson, Associate Professor of Marketing at London Business School, once described:

Most companies' approach to pricing as a 'mixture of voodoo and bingo.'

Generally, we buy emotionally and then justify rationally. Let me explain. Think back if you've bought a house or flat. How long did you take to decide 'this is the one?' Typical answers that people give me are from 10 seconds to a few minutes. Yet this is the biggest purchase or investment most of us ever make. It's our money yet we make such an important decision in less time than it takes us to decide what to choose on a restaurant menu.

Yet later in the process of house buying we then rationalise our reasons to friends and colleagues with logical arguments:

'It's near the station/shops/school/amenities.'

'It's a good investment.'

'There's scope for improvement.'

These are all our logical rational reasons.

In a business-to-business situation, there is a similar mixture of emotional and rational reasons for buying. Do not under-estimate the strength of the emotional reasons. We like to pretend that business decisions are so rational and logical. Most of us make decisions emotionally like Captain Kirk of Star Trek yet we like to think we make decisions on purely logical rational grounds like Mr Spock, the Vulcan.

> *It's unwise to pay too much, but it's worse to pay too little.*
>
> *When you pay too much, you lose a little money – that is all.*
>
> *When you pay too little, you sometimes lose everything, because the thing you bought was incapable of doing the thing it was bought to do.*
>
> *The common law of business balance prohibits paying a little and getting a lot – it can't be done.*
>
> *If you deal with the lowest bidder, it is well to add something for the risk you run. And if you do that, you will have enough to pay for something better.*
>
> *John Ruskin 1819-1900*
>
> (This was reproduced in *Campaign* magazine in 2010 as a full page ad with the caption 'Published in the interests of all suppliers everywhere'.)

The art and science of negotiating prices

Let's look at the key negotiation principles around pricing.

It is highly likely you are not charging enough compared to the value that your client is enjoying from your work! Many businesses tend to under-charge in relation to the value received. But what is a price? A price is not what someone charges, it is the amount someone is prepared to pay. If your client readily pays your price, you may not be charging enough.

Understand why the client has selected you to pitch for some work. If they have been recommended to use you, they may be more accepting of your price. If they see you as just the same as your competitors, then you will have difficulty justifying any price premium. Ideally, have an understanding of the client's budget, even just a guide, before stating your price.

The price you first charge a client will largely dictate the level of price you can charge for the rest of the relationship in the future.

Plan how you will frame your price. Before you talk about your price make sure you talk through the value the client will enjoy. Talk about the benefits, the likely results, the value, the 'afters' and the outcome before any mention of price.

The longer you take to say your price the more money you will make.

Conversely, the quicker you say your price the less money you will make. Once you have said your price people 'switch off listening.' Sometimes inexperienced sales people say their price too early and then afterwards try to justify it by talking about the value to be enjoyed. It's then too late. The client is thinking a variety of questions and thoughts to themselves such as: 'Can I afford it?' 'How does that compare?' 'Shall I go elsewhere?' 'How should I respond?' 'Is it good, bad, high, low?'

Aim your price or fee realistically high. Aim slightly higher than you feel 100% comfortable with. Stretch your comfort zone slightly. You may feel more confident to do this with a new client. Have a reason for where you have started. Be ready to give a rationale. Have three prices in your mind: an ideal, a target and a walk-away. You should have various concessions attached to each price level. Typically, we tend to have one price in our head and often there is no walk-away. The walk-away price is the most important one. It is much easier to come down in price than it is to go up.

I was talking to an agency who, in an e-auction, had dropped their fees by over £100,000 having been caught up in a bidding war. They had not considered and agreed internally their walk-away price before the e-auction.

Be prepared for your price – whatever it is, no matter how low – to be challenged. We haggle more readily in a car-boot sale than in a department store. Know how you will respond to those challenges. Anticipating your client's price challenge is important. This is a key part of your preparation. Plan your potential responses to their challenges.

Never apologise for your price – say your price with pride. Say it slowly, clearly and confidently. Confidence in stating your price is vital. (Sometimes the volume of our voice drops when stating our price or fee. This suggests lack of confidence in our price). As you say your price, watch their reaction.

Believe in your value and your price. People remember quality longer than they remember a high price. Conversely, they remember poor quality or poor results far longer and quickly forget the price they paid. The first person you must sell your price to is…YOU. If you lack confidence in your price then it is unlikely the client will feel confident in your price.

When you agree to a very tight deadline from a client there is a risk of compromising the quality of your work. When that happens, the client forgets the tight deadline and remembers the reduced quality of work and disappointing results. In that situation, give the client two prices: the first to complete the task to a normal deadline and the second a higher price to work to the very tight deadline. You may find the client can live with the later delivery date.

Increase your fees and rates regularly – minimum once a year at least to keep in line with inflation or, at worst, adjust/improve the profitability level of the account. Set up a fee diary which logs when each fee should be reviewed and also when the conversation should be first raised, perhaps three months in advance. This may also coincide with the client's budget planning for the following year. It is better to raise it early than after the client has submitted their budgets to their board.

Make the first purchase easy. That does not mean discount the first purchase. That simply creates a precedent which will be difficult to overcome further along the relationship. A guarantee reduces the risk of a first purchase. Buying a smaller quantity reduces the initial outlay and makes it an easier purchase.

Avoid round figures; £10,750 looks better than £10,000. £10,750 suggests there is a more detailed budget rather than the figure was plucked out of thin air.

Beware of on-the-spot pricing. Clients will often say they 'just want a ballpark' and that they 'won't hold you to it.' In my experience, they generally do hold you to it! If you are forced to give a ballpark figure, I would suggest giving a range of fee levels depending on the specific requirements the client chooses. These could be positioned as 'basic' and 'high value.' Explain any key assumptions you have made to gauge the price.

Clients try to commoditise agencies because it makes their life simpler, makes it harder for you to justify a premium price and increases the client's bargaining power. Avoid becoming commoditised. The more you become commoditised, the more your client will focus on price and buy on price.

There are three types of buyer:

- Those who buy premium-priced products – target them

- Those who buy on quality and value – target them

- Those who buy on price alone – avoid them

Clients will give you clues very quickly in the conversation with them for you to detect which type of buyer from the three above that they are. In my experience, the best and happiest clients are the ones who have paid full price. The most unhappy clients have been those who received a discount. The client's perception of you reduces as soon as you offer to lower your fee. Be prepared to lose customers who only want to pay the lowest price. Avoid bargain-basement clients. If your price appeals to everyone it is probably way too low for your best and most profitable clients.

- Higher prices suggest better quality and extra benefits. If you drop your price too much you can lose credibility, lose customers and commoditise your service.

- Choose your language carefully. Sell value, sell results, talk about ROI, investment, profit, payback and payback time.

- There are generally 10 differences for which clients are prepared to pay a premium:

  - Quality or perceived quality

  - Reliability

  - Certainty and reduced risk

  - Convenience

  - Tailoring

  - Emotion

  - Ease – less hassle

  - Specific differences

  - Consensus (lots of people are buying it so it must be good)

  - Scarcity

Price setting

There are four different approaches to setting a price. You may wish to consider a combination of these in assessing your fee levels.

1. Based on competitors' prices – you charge the 'industry norm' or the market rate.

2. Cost plus – you take your in-costs and add a margin to cover overheads and profit.

3. What will the market bear? Develop your price and see how the market responds. Then adjust accordingly.

4. Value-based fees – in relation to the value delivered. (My recommendation is to charge value-based fees. However, this is difficult now for agencies that have gone so heavily down the hourly and daily rates system of charging. Niche and boutique agency services can probably quote on value-based fees).

I heard a wonderful story about how to decide what price to charge a client which may or may not be true. Either way it is a great story and can be adapted to agencies.

Two shrewd brothers ran a company in North London which provides audiovisual equipment for conferences and major events. Whenever a quotation was required for a customer, each brother would go into his separate office and calculate the quotation and his justification for the price to be charged. Both brothers would then meet up and compare their different quotes and the justification for the price. They would always charge the higher figure, using the justification provided by the brother with the higher quote.

Could agencies have a similar approach? Two directors each propose the fee and justification to be charged for a scope of work. The highest fee is charged using the justification provided. When the higher fee is accepted by the client, the director with the lower fee buys the other one a good bottle of wine or lunch.

An interesting story comes from the pharmaceutical industry about pricing strategy that is counter-intuitive.

> *Some years ago, Glaxo were planning to launch Zantac (anti-ulcer drug) onto the market. They had to price Zantac against the established Tagamet (SmithKline) which was the number one brand at the time. The option of undercutting Tagamet's price was tempting and the obvious solution. Instead, Glaxo considered the benefits of Zantac over Tagamet (2 doses/day vs 4 doses/day and fewer side effects). They believed Zantac had considerable benefits over the established brand so they launched with a 50% price premium.*

> *The higher price drew attention to the differentiation. It challenged doctors to consider Zantac far more than if Glaxo had launched at a cheaper price. If they had launched Zantac at a discount to Tagamet the likely assumption by doctors would have been that Zantac was just a cheaper copy of the leading brand. So what happened? Sales of Zantac soared and profits went from £50m to £600m in five years.*

The dangers of discounting

Imagine selling a simple item which you buy for £8 and sell for £10. Your gross margin is £2 (20%) and if you sell 100 units you make a gross profit of £200.

Price you sell at	£10	
Cost to buy	£8	
Your gross margin	£2	
Units	100	
Gross profit	£200	

This is a very simple maths sum. Imagine now that your client puts pressure on you to drop your price. You drop your price by 10% to £9.

However, let's assume you are still buying the item at £8. Your gross margin has reduced to £1. In order to make the same gross profit you now have to sell 200 units – twice as many.

Price you sell at	£10	£9 (10% reduction)
Cost to buy	£8	£8
Your gross margin	£2	£1
Units	100	200 (twice as many)
Gross profit	£200	£200

This is the danger of discounting. A small change to the top line price has a major impact on the bottom line profit.

So how does this impact on agencies? Most agencies work on 10-15% profitability margin – some less, some higher. When you discount your fee even by 1% it can have a huge impact on your agency's profitability.

If you want to be highly profitable then charge a premium price for what you do. You had better, then, be the best at what you do, in fact you need to be world class. Be better than anyone else and deliver huge value for your clients.

Payment By Results (PBR)

This has become an increasingly popular method used to reward agencies. The basic idea is that specific measures or criteria are agreed between the client and agency. If the agency fails to achieve those criteria there is a penalty. If the agency achieves or exceeds the criteria there is a reward. This seems straightforward; however, there have been some problems which have arisen with PBR.

- Beware of allocating too much of your fee to PBR. I would suggest 5%, maximum 10%, of your fee is put at risk. Ensure that the balance, the 90-95% is still at an acceptable profit level for the agency.

- Ensure you are rewarded for criteria over which you have substantial control. If the measure is on ice-cream sales, then the weather will be a major influence on sales yet is something the agency has no influence over.

- There have been a few cases of clients reneging on paying the PBR bonus, in one case claiming that there had been no budget provision so there was no money available for payment.

- In some cases the agency has had to wait a long time for payment. In one case I know of, this was over 18 months so the agency's cash flow will be affected.

- In some cases it has proved to be very lucrative for the agency. I have a concern that if this happens there is a likelihood that the PBR is downgraded in the following year.

- Ensure it is agreed at a very senior level, i.e. board level at the client end, and is carefully drawn up and approved by the client and agency Finance Directors.

Splitting the difference

A common negotiation ploy is 'splitting the difference.' Beware of agreeing to split the difference on a fee reduction. We might want to be seen to be co-operating and striving to achieve a solution; however, the difference we split will come straight off our bottom line.

Handling price challenges

It is a basic human need to ensure we don't get a bad deal. When we are suspicious our natural tendency is to bargain. Our other tendency is to fear losing the deal. As a smart negotiator and as part of your preparation, you will have anticipated your price to be challenged and prepared some possible responses to the challenge. In case you haven't, here are some considerations and then some potential responses.

It is rare that a buying decision is only about price – unless you are in a commodity market, which as an agency you do not want. Focus on the value you are providing to the client rather than defending your price. Your value has nothing to do with the number of hours you worked. It is rumoured that John Lennon wrote *A hard day's night* in just a few minutes. Should he have been paid on the basis of his time?

Clients like to tell you that your price is too high. They never tell you the opposite. I wonder why. Don't immediately believe clients when they tell you that you are expensive. Often it is a knee-jerk reaction by them designed to elicit a price-cutting reaction. Sometimes clients are going through the motions and feel they need at least to have tried to challenge your price. If that's the case, if you have a reasonable first response to their price challenge the client may back off.

You may want to have two or three price options, giving the client choice and allowing you to trade different concessions and tradables. Choice seems to enable clients to feel in control.

Beware of breaking down your fee and budgets too far – this can lead to penny-pinching.

Silence is a powerful tool when your price is being challenged. Often the client is slightly nervous confronting your price so silence can make them even more uneasy. You will feel uncomfortable, too. Ten seconds of silence can feel twice as long as normal. Clients may use silence on you as well; this is designed to put you on the back-foot.

If you drop your price quickly and too readily when your client challenges it, there are two important implications. First, the client is likely to see your generosity as a weakness. Secondly, they are likely to think you are making so much money you can easily give away some of it. They now see you as untrustworthy, or worse as a crook.

Perversely, the more you drop your price the more they want you to drop it still further.

If your client tells you they have a cheaper alternative and that it is identical to your proposal, the client is telling you a lie. If they really had an identical proposal they'd choose the cheapest one and not bother to call you. What they really mean is that they have a <u>similar</u> proposal which is cheaper but <u>inferior</u> to yours, and will you match the lower price.

Never drop your fee or price without reducing the value in some way. Take out some value, e.g. 10% less of the planner's time, 10% less of the senior director's time. Or trade it for some valuable concessions from your wish list. Or re-package the deal.

Avoid negotiating fees and rates on the telephone. I have always found it preferable to negotiate fees face-to-face. The accepted wisdom amongst the negotiation experts is that on the phone the conversation tends to move more quickly, you cannot see the other party's body language and silence is even more awkward on the phone. There is a high risk that we agree to a deal on the phone which we then subsequently regret, by which time it is too late.

When your fee or price is challenged, there are a number of possible responses you can make. These can simply give you more time to think or, in some cases, actually quash the challenge. They vary in level of assertiveness.

A few of my favourites are:

- **There's a good reason why our price is higher. Our clients get results.** This is useful when the client is suggesting they can buy the same cheaper elsewhere. It is a very confident response, suggesting the alternative may be cheaper but that the client will enjoy superior results with you.

- **Putting price aside for a moment, is this what you want?** This refocuses the client onto the proposal and benefits they will receive, rather than focusing solely on the price. When you go back through the proposal, the client often 'falls in love' with the proposal.

- **On what basis is it so expensive?** This gives you time to think and ask the client confidently to explain their rationale. Often there is no sound basis that the client can give you for justifying why they can say 'you are so expensive.'

One of my clients, a London-based agency, pitched for some business to an existing client. They were advised by the client that they had the best strategic thinking, the best creative approach and the best expertise to deliver the project. However, their price was substantially more than the other company who the client was appointing onto the project. The agency asked the client how much cheaper the other agency was. "90% cheaper," the client explained. "Are you comparing like with like?" asked the agency, "Who are they?" The client replied, "You won't have heard of them, they are based in Romania."

We are living in a global economy. Competitors aren't just in the UK. They can be in China, India, Brazil, Africa or Eastern Europe. There are many countries where the day-rate can be substantially less than in the UK or US. Time zones can work to their advantage, offering potentially a 24-hour service. How will you compete with that? The simple answer is you can't compete financially. However, you can compete by ensuring your expertise, your strategic thinking and, ultimately, the results you deliver exceed those of your competitors and the expectations of your client.

By the way, there is a happy end to the above story. The client came back to the London agency. The agency in Romania made mistakes resulting in the project de-railing and running late. However, this situation won't always happen. In time, the agency in Romania will improve its processes and quality of work.

- Imagine you run a restaurant. There are only two different dishes on the menu: Fillet Steak and Hamburger, selling at £16 and £8 respectively. Of course, some customers will want the Fillet Steak for the price of a Hamburger. Is it right to start charging £8 for the Fillet Steak? In fact if you do start offering Fillet Steak for only £8, customers are likely to be suspicious and think that either:

  - They get a small portion: It's a very small piece of Fillet Steak (about ½ size)

  - It's a substitute: It's not Fillet Steak. It's something masquerading as Fillet Steak, perhaps donkey?

  - It's poor quality: It's been sitting in the fridge for weeks and about to be thrown away

  - You're insane: you don't know how to run a restaurant and won't be in business for long

Don't sell Fillet Steak for the price of a burger.

Charge what you are worth not what the client will pay.

What if the pricing challenge by your client continues and is aggressive and determined?

Sometimes clients and Procurement will put huge pressure on you to reduce fees, rates and costs. In this situation you must be even better prepared.

- Be clear on your ideal, target and walk-away price. At what point are you prepared to say 'no?' The more prepared you are to say 'no' the more likely you are to achieve your goal in the long run.

- How important is this project/client to you? What is the longer-term potential of this client? If the client is a major proportion of your business, it makes objective decisions to walk-away very difficult. Conversely, if there is long-term potential, remember the precedents you might be about to set for yourself.

- Remind the client of your expertise, experience and results delivered for other similar clients.

- If you do decide to concede some ground then do not just give money away, always take some value out. Will the client like it? No, but the priority is about building a profitable and sustainable business, not necessarily about pleasing Procurement. Imagine you are in your local supermarket and are at the checkout to pay for your shopping and the cashier asks for £100. You explain that you only have £90. The cashier with no hesitation says, "What do you want to take out? Shall we take this item out or this one?" I recommend the same approach with your clients when they claim to not have enough money. The worst thing you could do is to provide the equivalent of £100 of shopping for £90. (Guess what the customer will want next week)?

- Do not try to keep clients by dropping your price. The damage you do will be deep and will cause you long-term problems.

- If you do decide to price-match for the client then trade something else such as payment terms, notice period, a year's contract or a certain level of monthly spend. Don't simply price-match a competitor. Deals are rarely just about price and if it is, what are you doing providing a commodity service?

What if the pressure from your client or Procurement turns into threats?

The ultimate sanction is, 'If you don't drop your prices/fees we will be forced to put the business out to pitch,' and 'If you don't drop your prices/fees you will be blacklisted from working with our company again.'

This is a horrible situation to be in. Several of the agencies I work with have had this type of threat from their clients. Ultimately you must decide how you want to respond to this type of threat. Some thoughts:

- Any client who resorts to threats and emotional blackmail is not seeking a partnership relationship with you. They want a 'master-slave' relationship. Is that the kind of relationship you want? If you enter this kind of relationship you will find that your self-belief and confidence will be eroded over time. When the other party gets what they want, their threatening behaviour won't stop. The relationship won't suddenly get better after you have given in to their threats. It will continue in the same way.

You get the behaviour that you tolerate.

- As tough as it may seem walking away from an abusive relationship, it is preferable long term to remaining in the relationship. Perversely, the more you are put under pressure may suggest they really want your work but believe that by using threatening behaviour they can get what they want.

- A question to those of you with children. If you give in to every demand your child makes – a pizza, a DVD, a late night, more time on the computer game, more sweets, an ice-cream, a Big Mac – what will you create for yourself as a parent? A monster! Sometimes as parents we have to exhibit 'tough love.' This is when, as parents, we make decisions which are for the long-term benefit of both parties. In the short term, there is some pain associated with 'tough love' for both the parent and child.

- I understand that the AAR estimated a few years ago the cost to a client of moving agency to be around £50,000. This took into account the time to visit prospective new agencies, brief them, view their responses, the disruption as a new agency learns the ropes and idiosyncrasies of the business, the cost of a few mistakes in the early days etc. Is it really in the client's best interest to put the business out to pitch on a whim?

- I would suggest a calm and assertive conversation with the client along the lines of, 'I understand your determination to reduce our prices; however, we are unable to reduce them. These are our normal rates we charge our other clients. These have been established to offer considerable value to our clients and provide a sensible and competitive return to us as a business. We enjoy working with you and have developed some excellent work (give several examples) which have achieved amazing results (give several examples). If you can agree to our fees/prices then we can get on with the business of building your brand, your business and your profits.' Clients continue working with agencies when they deliver the results they require.

  - Before your conversation with Procurement, understand from your marketing client how valuable your work has been for them.

- Tackling a problem like this is one of the tougher ones in business. Your satisfaction at resolving the issue in the right way will be immense and will show you that it is right to take a firm assertive approach – a front-foot mindset.

Our next challenge is how we can increase our fees and rates to existing clients. The longer we don't increase our fees to clients, the harder it becomes to do so. This is the subject of the next chapter.

CHAPTER 7

Charging higher fees

Key learnings

- The thorny subject of increasing the fees your clients pay

- The implications of not increasing your fees

- The implications of increasing your fees

- How best to do it

Beware of presenting budgets which are unprofitable for the agency or pitching your price too low.

Let me give you a warning. If you really want to increase your fees with some of your clients then it's like making an omelette. You can't make an omelette without breaking some eggs. You can't increase your fees without making some changes and affecting the relationship with your client – often the relationship can be enhanced in a positive way if you plan the detail. However, there is a risk you may also upset some of your clients.

Please do not bother reading this chapter unless you are prepared to put the effort into the preparation.

By reading the rest of this chapter you are deemed to have agreed to the condition of ruthless preparation. This is not a quick-fix action.

If you don't increase your fees to existing clients there are several dangers:

- As your costs increase, unless you are working more efficiently your profits will reduce

- The client will think you are weak and possibly desperate for their business

- Your self-confidence and self-belief will reduce. You are more likely to move towards a position of 'buyer-supplier' and away from 'trusted adviser'

- In a year's time the issue will be even greater and you will have missed out on whatever increased profitability you might have achieved if you had started on this mission now

- Teams working on unprofitable accounts are normally de-motivated

If you do increase your fees there are several different dangers:

- You may put your costs more under the spotlight

- The client or their Procurement department may look for alternative providers at a lower cost

- The client may price compare and benchmark your prices

- You may even lose some clients

So only increase your fees if you are delivering immense value, outstanding results, enabling your clients to overcome their most challenging business problems or have expertise which the client really needs or can't get easily elsewhere.

The benefits of higher fees can easily outweigh the previous dangers:

- It can reinforce to the client how good you are

- It can mean you must raise your game and increase the value your client experiences from you

- It can move you into a different position in the market, dealing with different and more senior clients

Increasing fees with new clients

The best place to start when you want to increase your fees generally is with new clients. Firstly you can test their reaction one at a time. You can craft your value story and your differentiation positioning from competitors. You may want to consider increasing fees when the prospect is a referral and is already 'part sold' on you. Increase your fees when you have recently won some new business or won a big new project from an existing client and you are feeling more bullish. If you generate more new business opportunities than you need, it makes it easier to increase your fee level. Increase fees when your confidence is on the rise.

I recently asked a sales person when she found it best to increase her prices. She paused and said, "When I don't care." I probably looked puzzled. She went on to explain what she meant about not caring. She felt that if she didn't mind about winning that new client because they were small, not a priority prospect or she was 'over-target' for the quarter, she was more confident to propose a higher than normal level of fee.

Whether you are over-target or not, THINK that you are over-target. Be in a positive 'over-target' mindset.

Increasing fees with existing clients

This has to be done even more carefully. Do it after your confidence is on the rise from increasing fees with new clients as previously described. Then decide which client to tackle first. Take one client at a time. I would recommend taking the least profitable client to increase fees first as your pilot study. The risk is least.

Preparation is vital. As part of your preparation, review the agency's current financial situation with this client. Understand why profitability is low with this client. Is it because of overall low fees, low rates, scope creep, over-servicing, poor account management, higher than normal re-works, poor briefings or poor brief-taking?

Review the timesheets. Where is the time mainly being spent and even wasted? Is too much senior time being spent on this client?

What actions can you take to improve profitability before you even talk to the client? How do your rates compare to market levels and other clients?

Revisit the original contract. Often over time, the work has changed and the agency hasn't identified this change. What did the original contract or agreement state? If it was written and agreed several years earlier, quite often the contract now has little or no resemblance to the current situation.

Talk to the team. Find out their perspective from a day-to-day point of view. How motivated is the team?

How important is this client to us in terms of size, sector experience, relationship, credibility etc? Gather information from the client about how they see your value and contribution to their business. Ask questions casually that can help you in your assessment of the situation and planning how to structure the conversation.

What financial situation do you want to aim for with this client? Over what time period? What has to happen for this to be achieved? Perhaps aim for a small increase initially with the principle of another increase in six months. Focus on improving profitability of a client rather than necessarily increasing the overall fee. Besides the fee, what else is on your wish list with this client?

Agree with your senior management your approach and ensure their full support and commitment. Keep them apprised of progress and your thinking so they can support you. (There is nothing worse than a client complaining to your boss about you wanting to increase their fees and your boss contradicting and over-ruling you. You will need your boss and senior management colleagues to support you completely).

Put yourself in the client's shoes. See the issue from their perspective. Imagine you are the other party. What's important to you? What's valuable? What is a 'must have?' What is a 'like to have?' What are your concerns? What are the risks or perceived risks? What is causing them the most 'pain' in their business? What are their biggest problems and how can you help them even more with those issues? How can your solutions reduce their pain and problems? What is the cost of those problems? How much do they need you? What options do they have? What is their BATNA? Often the client is aware they are getting a bargain. They realise that a comparable agency will charge a similar price to this new desired fee level.

Choose your timing carefully to raise the subject of a fee increase. There's never a right time to increase fees, only times that are slightly better than others. Decide when is a good time to sow seeds – perhaps after a particularly successful project has been completed and the results exceed the client's expectation. Tread carefully by sounding the client out first. Depending on their reaction when you sowed the seeds, decide how you wish to proceed.

Rehearse how you plan to raise the subject and anticipate the likely response, questions and objections. In your rehearsal, ask a colleague to act as the client in the role of devil's advocate, firing difficult questions at you and challenging your proposal. Plan and craft the detail of the wording of your potential responses to their objections and questions.

At the meeting with the client, take a colleague, someone not involved directly on the account, to provide a more objective perspective. Your Finance Director can add credibility and objectivity. Ensure you are both 'on the same page' by planning well in advance so there is no chance of contradiction between you at the meeting with the client. One of you can take the role of good cop while the other takes the role of bad cop. Turn your metaphorical antennae up to full sensitivity. Listen carefully to their responses, their language, watch their body language, and watch their eye contact. Use your intuition. Review the work, the results and the value derived by the client over the previous six to twelve months with the client so they are reminded of the benefits you provide. Monetise that value to the client compared to the investment made with your company. Make it as tangible as possible. Project one, two, three years into the future the likely increased value and results the client can expect to receive.

Ensure you are in the right state of mind for the meeting. Any sense of desperation on your part will be quickly detected by the client. Seek a win-win solution so both parties are feeling satisfied. Give fee options, maximum three from the choice below:

- Same team, increased fee

- Reduced team/workload, very slight increase in fee

- More reduced team, same fee

Put a deadline in place to resolve the situation, otherwise there is a risk the client is slow to respond and avoids the issue. I've had agencies tell me they have been left in limbo for three months, even six months, after submitting a fee increase proposal, waiting for the client to respond and give feedback.

Hold your nerve. Be prepared to say 'no.' (In nearly every case, whenever my agency clients have said 'no' to their clients and are prepared to walk away, the other party has softened and agreed to the deal). What's your BATNA (Best Alternative to a Negotiated Agreement)? What's their likely BATNA? Think through what you will do if you don't get the fee increase you are after. What options do you have?

Review progress and your learnings. What have you learnt for next time? How will you handle it differently next time? Share the experience with colleagues. When you have achieved a successful outcome, move on to the next low profitability client and start the process again.

What do you do if the client will agree a smaller fee increase than requested? It is your business decision and is a commercial judgment. I would suggest you respond by saying, "If you can only pay £x then we will have to reduce..." If they are close to your proposed new fee level, you could consider splitting the difference or trading.

What options do we have if the client refuses to increase the fee? Accept for a specified period after which the topic will be discussed again. This may coincide with their new financial year to allow the client to build the increase into the following year's budgets. This may help the client in their planning process. If the client is amenable to this, it at least indicates a willingness to improve the situation. Change the make-up of the team to a lower overhead base (reducing the hours of, or removing from the team, a particularly valuable member of the team will get attention but can be a risky option). Reduce the hours of the senior team on this client's business. Consider targeting a competitor of the client (after all, you have a wealth of experience to offer). Or resign the client if profitability is so untenable; this is the final option when all else has failed.

One of the great tools to use when negotiating is to ask well-crafted questions. These will certainly be helpful when pushing for an increase in fee levels. The next chapter will help you plan and craft your high-quality negotiation questions.

CHAPTER 8

That's a good question

Key learnings

- The Power of Questions and the importance of planning your questions in advance

- The difference between an ordinary and a high-quality question

- Examples of great questions to ask in different situations

How well do you prepare for negotiations?

Do you 'wing it'?

Great questions are vital in business and especially in negotiations. Before we look at specific questions, let's be clear about what great questions are, why we ask them and how they help us.

"You can tell the quality of the question by the quality of the answer it gets". David Frost

Great questions:

- Should always have a purpose for being asked

- Should be planned in advance

- Generate useful information

- Can uncover hidden agendas

- Can enhance your expertise

- Can build rapport, especially when combined with good listening skills

- Can give you time to think when a discussion stalls

The best questions are typically open questions, usually starting with who, what, why, where, when, how and tell me (I appreciate 'tell me' isn't a question but it achieves a similar end result). From a neuro-science point of view, open questions typically generate far greater activity in the brain than closed questions. Try it yourself. Ask yourself, 'Where did I go for my last holiday?' For most of us this is a simple question generating a simple short answer. Generally, a question beginning with 'where' is an open question but in this example it generates a short answer and is more closed than open. Then ask yourself, 'Which was my favourite holiday?' For most of us this will generate a much deeper consideration and longer answer, giving more information and insights into us and our preferences. Often we will scour through our mental files considering a selection of holidays over the years in order to select our 'favourite' and the specific reason(s).

How do you know when you've asked a great question? There are a few clues. The person may pause while they take time to think about their answer. They may say, 'that's a good question' or may even repeat the question while they think through the answer. You want clients to think 'wow, these people are on the ball. I like how they think. They will help me shine.'

In contrast, if your questions are being answered with little or no hesitation, there is a good possibility you are asking predictable questions and ones which have already been asked several times before by your competitors. What does the predictability of your questions say about your work – predictable perhaps? This is hardly likely to excite the other party.

Take time to craft your questions. Crafting and asking great questions is a core skill of great consultants and trusted advisers.

Care must be taken when asking questions. The other party must not feel they are being interrogated. The questions must be conversational, natural and have a logical flow. Openness and a willingness to answer questions come with a reasonable level of trust between the two parties. For real trust to exist, the client must believe that you have their best interests at heart. I would recommend explaining to the client why you are asking these various questions, such as, 'I have a few questions to ask which will help me truly understand your issues and help me develop a great robust proposal for you. Is it OK for me to start asking you some questions?'

Often the simplest questions can be very powerful and open up the other party. I was running a workshop on questioning skills with a group of Fund Managers for a leading financial investment company. One of the most successful Fund Managers explained that his favourite first question to ask a CEO or Finance Director was simply 'How's business?' This simple, apparently innocent question opened up the conversation with the other party. The Fund Manager went on to explain that how the question was answered told him lots about the focus and priorities of the CEO.

Follow-on questions are useful. This is when the next question drills deeper on the same topic as the previous question. Once, when working with a team of Recruitment Consultants and observing their questioning styles with candidates, I noticed how the best consultants asked several follow-on questions on the same topic before moving to another topic. The other consultants seemed to bounce from one question topic to the next like a butterfly flitting from flower to flower. Which was more effective? The former took a little more time but they seemed to gain a far deeper understanding of the candidate, their true talents and abilities. The latter seemed more 'efficient' on the surface but nowhere near as effective.

Trust is an important element to ensure the client is candid with you. Sometimes questions can appear aggressive or too assertive, especially in times of emotion or friction. 'Why' can be heard by the other party as questioning their ability or decision-making. You can soften a question by prefacing it with phrases such as:

'Can I ask about..?'

'I'm wondering whether..?'

'I'm curious about..?'

'Would I be right in saying..?'

'So I understand better..?'

'This may be a stupid question but..?'

Taking time to craft high-quality questions is highly advisable. A few moments turning a good or average question into a great question is time well spent.

Is there really such a difference in the quality of questions?

You may remember in one of the Pink Panther movies, Peter Sellers as Inspector Clouseau, the bungling French detective, enters an apartment block. He sees a man leaning against a wall and a dog nearby. Clouseau asks the question, "Does your dog bite?" To which the man simply replies "No.." Clouseau leans forward and pats the dog. The dog bites him. Annoyed, Clouseau says to the man, "I thought you said your dog does not bite," to which the man shrugs and replies, "That's not my dog."

Clouseau had thought he was asking a useful question but could have asked a much better question: "Is that your dog; does it bite?"

Often what the client doesn't say is as useful as what they do say. Do they answer your question or a different one? What do they leave out? What can you hear 'between the lines?' Did you observe a change in body language when you asked a particular question? Did they avert their eyes from you? Was there an awkward pause after a specific question? Are their answers just the bare minimum or were they generous and complete in their answers, holding nothing back?

Given that negotiating takes place at all the different 'life-stages' of a client-agency relationship, from networking to first meeting to pitching to break-up, let's look at the different 'life-stages' and then some relevant example questions for each stage.

Networking questions

These questions are for use at the very early stage of the relationship and are designed to identify general business opportunities and build rapport. They need to be used particularly subtly while the relationship is still in its early stage and trust is growing slowly. They should be broad – especially to start becoming more focused as the conversation progresses and relationship develops. They may be used in a networking situation at a conference or seminar, for example.

- Tell me about your business

- How are you finding business at the moment?

- What are the major challenges you are facing this year?

Initial new business meeting with the prospect

This stage is about determining the potential of the business in terms of size, relevance to our expertise, urgency, seriousness and legitimacy.

In short, you want questions to qualify the opportunity.

- What exactly are you looking for ideally?
- How important is this issue/need for you, on a scale of 1-10?
- What areas of improvement are you looking for?
- What is the cost of the problem?
- What are the implications for the business if you don't address this issue?

Stealing business from competitors

This is when the prospective client explains they are unhappy with their existing provider.

- Is there any particular reason you use…..?
- Do you have a back-up provider?
- What influenced your decision?

Finding the right decision-maker and buyer

It is vital to ensure we are in discussion with the person who makes the decision or agency appointment. You do not want to find that you have invested considerable time only to discover they were getting the information 'for their boss' or have no decision-making ability, besides the ability to say 'no.' However, gate-keepers can be influential so care must be taken to not alienate them.

In tough economic times it is common for the traditional decision-maker to become just the gate-keeper. The authority for spending money moves up one or two levels (your day-to-day contact is unlikely to tell you this). Just because someone has a budget, do not assume they have authority to spend it. Increasingly they have to gain approval to spend the budget from a higher authority.

e whether the potential work is worth your effort
relevant to your expertise. The larger the client
ple are involved in the buying decision.

..1at will be the approval process for a project like this and for this level of budget spend?

- Who else, besides you, would be involved in the decision-making process?

- Whose budget will support this initiative?

- If you wanted to proceed with this project, who else would you need to discuss this with?

Questions when being briefed by the client

Taking a brief is so important. In my early days in agency life I took most briefs at face value and seldom questioned them sufficiently. I assumed they were written by the 'expert', i.e. the client. However, I then realised that often client's briefs are poorly written and not well thought through. Verbal briefs are particularly dangerous. They give the client too much 'wiggle-room.' Verbal briefs can send you off in the wrong direction and the priorities can be misunderstood. Written briefs force the client to think through their priorities and give some order to their thinking. Push for written briefs wherever possible from the client. As a last resort, you should turn the client's verbal brief into a written brief which they subsequently approve and sign off.

If you do receive a poor brief then it is your job to turn that poor brief into a good brief. On the plus side, this can give you a distinct competitive advantage in a pitch or competitive situation as you are now working to a better and tighter brief than your competitors.

Three key areas of questions for any brief are:

1. Objective

2. Value/success

3. Measurement

Gather clear objectives

- What are the most important results you are focused on?

- What are the biggest opportunities you want to take advantage of?

- What are the biggest challenges you face?

Establish the value worth investing in

- What would achieving these objectives be worth?

- What would be really valuable? What else? What would success look like? Which is the most important? And the next?

- What will happen if you do nothing?

Monetise the success or value of your activity. Encourage the client to specify a monetary value. In the US the term is 'dollarise.' Many clients will avoid doing this. Perhaps they feel it is tying them down too specifically. However, it has huge benefits to you, and ultimately to the client. It keeps you focused on the real priorities and ensures the budget is appropriate to the requirements of success. High value comes from the client's perspective, not your assumptions of their requirements. Take time to establish what is high value to your client.

Define the measures of success, the metrics by which your activity will be judged

The measures may be a mix of objective quantitative ones plus some subjective qualitative ones. Push for at least one of the former.

- What criteria will you use to measure our success?

- What measures will tell you our work has been successful and effective?

- What are the most important measures you will use to gauge success?

- How well are your current measures of success working?

When I talk through these three key areas – objective, success, measurement – sometimes people ask if I've forgotten the all-important question of budget. Don't ask about budget until the three key areas have been clearly articulated and agreed. Why wait till now? To help position how realistic the budget is versus the task to be achieved and the ROI. Only then, ask about the budget.

Budget questions

These are questions to gain greater clarity around the level of the budget, the flexibility and the potential for increase.

- How much flexibility is there in the budget? (This helps to identify if the budget is rigid or can be increased for the right idea and potential upside).

- Under what circumstance would the budget increase?

- What are your criteria to decide how to allocate your budget? Would you be happy if I provided a variety of options, some at a higher level of budget?

General ongoing client questions

- How has business/your role/the market/customers changed over the past few years?

- What are your biggest challenges? What are the biggest challenges you face in growing your business? What keeps you awake at night?

- What are the most (un)profitable parts of your business?

- If the marketing Fairy Godmother granted you one business wish, what would it be?

Questions to help you decide whether to respond to a tender

There are some key questions to ask early on in the tender process to help you decide whether to 'go/not go' for a specific tender. In essence, you are trying to assess the probability of you winning the tender over and above the quality of your actual submission.

1. **How many other companies are responding to this tender?** I have heard of tenders with over 100 agencies submitting a response. Avoid these situations unless you have an existing relationship with the client organisation and have 'the inside track.' If not then your chance of winning is highly remote.

2. **Of the companies tendering, how many have you worked with before?** If your company has never worked with the client and the client has worked a lot with several competitors, your probability to win is substantially reduced.

3. **What are your selection criteria for deciding how to award the business?** How clearly are these criteria identified? Are they weighted? Do they play to your strengths? How clearly does the client articulate these criteria? Some clients refuse to share their criteria.

4. **We have some specific questions to ask your....sales director, marketing manager, PR manager – can we talk to them?** If they won't let you speak to a particular decision-maker this suggests they are more interested in your price than forming a business relationship with you.

5. **Ask other general questions about the tender.** If the client is not forthcoming with the information it may suggest they are not really interested in a business relationship, simply your price. (Sometimes government organisations are forbidden to provide additional information or, if they do provide extra information, their answers must be made available to every company tendering.)

    The overall responsiveness of the client organisation to answering your questions will give a strong clue to their openness and how they would behave as a client.

    Tenders are a huge investment of time for agencies. Decide carefully whether to invest the time (often over 30-40 hours).

Questions on your agency's service and how happy the client is

Most of us avoid conflict and confrontation. Both the agency and client avoid sensitive areas. If the client is unhappy about your agency's work it is better to learn this as early as possible. Don't expect the problem to go away. Problems seldom go away. Typically, problems grow into bigger problems. Ask penetrating questions regularly to give you a sense of how delighted the client is, or isn't. Right at the start of the relationship, advise the client you plan to ask questions regularly about their sense of satisfaction because you want them to be delighted, to feel they are with the best agency for their requirements and they feel sufficiently 'loved' by the agency.

- How can we deliver even more value for your business this year/

next year?

- What do we need to do to win your 'Agency of the Year' award? (They probably won't have one so you can simply smile and say, 'but if you did have one, would we win it? If so, why? If not, why?' It's a fun and light-hearted way to assess how the client really feels).

- Why did you choose us and are we delivering to those original criteria?

The Ultimate Question

'Would you be prepared to recommend us as an agency to friends and colleagues?'

This question is inspired by Fred Reichheld in his book The Ultimate Question. This question is used to generate the NPS or Net Promoter Score. The NPS is claimed by Fred and many others to be one of the best predictors and indicators of business success. Fred's actual question is, 'How likely is it that you would recommend this company to a friend or colleague?'

Questions to identify if all is not well!

Has your meeting frequency with the client reduced? Are they returning your calls as readily? Are they more critical than before? Does your intuition tell you all is not well? Client criticism is more valuable than gold. It's a 'Moment of Truth.' Bill Gates believes 'your most unhappy clients are your greatest source of learning'.

You may need to preface these questions to give the client permission to air their concerns, such as, 'We are human and sometimes don't always get everything right. I'm keen to understand if there are any areas where you feel frustrated or where you feel we aren't achieving your expectations. I really would appreciate your openness and honesty.' This is another important time to watch their body language. Do they shuffle uncomfortably? Do they look away? Do they look pensive and anxious?

- Can I have some honest feedback?

- What concerns, if any, do you have with us/our work/the team?

- Nothing is perfect. What's the one thing that irritates or frustrates you or your people about us?

- If you and I swapped jobs tomorrow, what would be the top three things you'd do differently or improve?

Then watch their body language, listen to their words, watch their eyes.

'Elephant in the room' questions

These are the question(s) we really need to ask but we avoid. We know we should ask the question but either we don't want to hear the answer or are embarrassed to ask the question. Either ask the question or tackle the issue indirectly. Don't sweep it under the carpet hoping it will go away – it won't.

Scenario 1: The client thinks you are expensive.

You may believe the client thinks you are expensive because of your company name, office location or profile. It may be a serious problem and may even prevent them awarding you the work. Don't ignore it. Ask the question.

'Some clients feel we may be expensive because of.... Would that be true of you? We certainly aren't the cheapest but what we pride ourselves on is achieving results, providing great value and helping our clients perform ahead of their marketplace and competitors.'

Scenario 2: The client is concerned about your capabilities or experience in some way.

'You may be wondering how we will manage your business across Europe/the US/Far East. Is that a concern? Let me explain how we plan to cover this.'

Scenario 3: A new business pitch may be a possible conflict with an existing client. (This is a frequent dilemma for agencies. Clients want you to have experience in their sector but direct conflict may be a problem for them. Do we raise it early on and risk being excluded or do we wait and hope the problem resolves itself, which it rarely does?)

One agency I have advised works with a leading confectionery manufacturer. The agency was approached by a major competitor of the client to do some work. The agency agonised over the decision and said to the prospect, "We already work with ABC and have real insight and understand this sector exceedingly well. Might this cause you any concern? Can we find a way to resolve this?"

The prospect expressed their delight at the agency's honesty and how this demonstrated the potential for real trust between the prospective client and the agency. The prospect awarded the agency a sizeable programme of work in another non-conflicting part of their business (this saved years of 'hoping the client never finds out!')

Some years ago I worked with a new start-up healthcare agency to advise them regarding their business development. They told me about a recent competitive pitch they had made to a major blue-chip healthcare company. They invested considerable time, effort and money into this hugely important potential new client. After the pitch, the client advised them their strategic thinking was the best, their creative solution was the best, the team was the best and even their prices and costs were the best. However, they couldn't award them the work as they had a policy of requiring three years of trading accounts. The agency had been going only six months. The agency didn't want to ask the 'elephant in the room' question 'We've been trading successfully for only six months; is that likely to cause a problem if you wanted to award us the work?' They didn't ask because they didn't want to raise it as a potential problem and they didn't want to hear the possible answer. I believe it is generally better to raise the potential problem before investing several weeks of effort into a pitch you can ultimately never win.

Price challenge questions asked by clients

Questions are very useful when your price, fees or rates are being questioned, challenged or compared to competitors. Questions will give you time to think, show your confidence, help you in remaining calm and on the front-foot, not the back-foot. Because this is likely to be a sensitive area, you may want to select those responses you feel most comfortable with, depending on the situation at hand. Think carefully about the tone of how you say these responses.

- That's the price

- There's a good reason for that, our clients get results

- Putting price aside, is this what you want?

- On what basis is it expensive?

Tackling tough client questions

Clients sometimes ask us tough questions which catch us unaware. The benefit of this next section is to give you time to think about how best to respond to a tough client question or even delay answering the question.

Beware of showing the 'flinch' which shows you were caught off-guard. One of the best ways to avoid being caught off-guard is to anticipate the likely tough questions that clients ask generally. Brainstorm the likely tough questions clients may ask you on this particular project or campaign. This is a key part of your preparation. Prepare your answers to these tough questions – this will aid your confidence. Never answer until you clearly understand the client's question.

Before answering a client's tough question, think through what's behind their question. There is always a reason behind why a question has been asked. Work out what the reason is. What are they really asking? What is the real question behind their question? What is the intent behind their question?

To give you more time to think and decide how best to tackle a tough question asked by a client, there are several stalling techniques:

- Ask questions to clarify their question

- Repeat their question

- Say 'That's an interesting question. What makes you ask that?'

- 'What specifically is it that you want to know?'

- 'I need to think about that (or I need to give that some thought). Let me get back to you with my thoughts within 24 hours.'

- 'I don't know the answer. I will get back to you within 24 hours.'

- Briefly answer their tough question and then bridge to the point you really want to make.

- If you want to evade answering a question, provide an answer to a question that was not asked but touches on the relevant topic (this may be risky if the client spots what you are doing).

'Sorry, what did you say?'

Sometimes, when asking the client questions we can be so focused on planning the next question or thinking further ahead that we forget to actually listen to their answer to our original question. We can get distracted and lose our train of thought. There are several problems associated with this. Firstly, we may miss some vital information. Secondly, when others see we are only half-listening they tend to close down and rapport reduces. So they may be less forthcoming with additional information.

How good are you at listening? London Business School carried out a study where they asked senior executives to rate themselves on a series of capabilities. Their colleagues were then asked to rate the same individual on those same skills. The capability with the biggest disparity was 'listening skills.' People typically rated themselves much higher on listening ability than their colleagues rated them.

People hear what they want to hear.

Let me ask you again – How good are you at listening?

When you are listening to yourself talking it is difficult to hear what the other person is saying.

Listening skills are a crucial part of questioning skills. We need full body active listening. There are a range of signals which show our client we are actively listening. This in turn builds rapport and encourages the client to tell us even more. Giving a person 'a good listening to' is one of the best things you can do to another human being.

Certainly, a wonderful clue that you are in rapport and the client is telling you so much is when the client says, 'I shouldn't really be telling you this, but...'

Active listening skills

- You will never lose a sale by listening too much – talking too much, you bet.

- Eye contact builds trust and rapport.

- Smiling and nodding in agreement. Smiling is a powerful way to connect.

- 'Ah-ha' noises suggesting agreement and encourages the speaker to continue.

- Leaning forward enthusiastically shows your interest level.

- Supplementary questions, which build on their previous answer(s), show you are thinking about what the other party is saying.

- Making written notes shows respect for the information and reassures the client that the information is also important to you.

- Summarising and paraphrasing your understanding demonstrates you were listening. This serves as a useful wrap-up at the end and may generate further information.

If you want to develop your listening skills further then consider these points:

- Beware of hearing what you want to hear. It is easy to be selective and filter the content.

- Talk less, listen more. You will learn more when you are listening.

- Turn up the sensitivity of your 'antennae' to pick up those subtle yet important clues and buying signals.

- Listen to their use of language:

- Where is the emotion when they speak? Use their language back to them. How confident do they sound? Are they using fillers ('ums, erhs') or is their language weakening their position ('sort of', 'you know', 'kind of')?

- Our language gives away lots of clues about how we think. What is their language primarily about:

  - People or things

  - Big picture or detail

  - Away from or towards

  - Thinking or feeling

  - I/me or us/we?

- It's not about what's right or wrong, it's an illustration of how they think. The more you tune into and use your client's language, the greater will be the connection between you and the client.

Questions to help you become more consultative with clients

I recommend when you next meet with your clients that you ask three simple questions:

1. What is it that you like and value that we, the agency, do?

2. What one improvement could we make that would help your business?

3. How can we help you improve how you achieve your goals next year?

The answers to these questions are generally highly enlightening and, as well as providing useful information, tend to improve the quality of the client-agency relationship.

Do not assume you know the answers to these questions.

Your client's words and phrases in answer to these questions, especially to the first question, are enlightening and ideal for use in new business situations as well as with existing clients. The words and phrases that your clients use to answer the first question will generally resonate with other prospective clients.

In addition to your clients, there are often other stakeholders involved in agency negotiations. These may be our colleagues and our suppliers with whom we need to negotiate. This is the subject of the next chapter.

CHAPTER 9

Internal negotiations and supplier negotiations

Key learnings

- How to apply your negotiation skills and techniques effectively with your colleagues

- How to apply your negotiation skills and techniques effectively with your suppliers

Some agency people tell me they find internal negotiations more confrontational than negotiations with clients. Some agency people also find it hard to negotiate with long-standing suppliers with whom they have built close working relationships.

Internal negotiations

Develop your friends before you need them.

An Italian delegate told me this quote once in a workshop. It is so appropriate to internal negotiations with colleagues and other departments in the agency. It seems that negotiating with colleagues and especially with other departments in larger agencies is harder than negotiating with the client.

As agency structure has generally become flatter and disciplines more specialised, our ability to work collaboratively with colleagues has become increasingly important. Added to that is working with network colleagues in other offices and in other countries. Agency people need an MBA in Collaboration.

I have seen clumsy, ill-prepared and poorly-planned account handlers upset a couple of creatives with their attitude and poor briefing. It has then taken the account handler many months to regain the respect and co-operation of the whole of the creative department. That's a long time to eat humble pie.

How can we improve our ability to negotiate effectively with our internal colleagues? (You may have a sense of déjà vu with client negotiations).

• **Treat your colleagues in other departments as peers, not as your servants**

Involve them in the client's business. Share and discuss your plans. Ask their advice. Ask how they prefer to be briefed. Then invest time in your briefs and briefings. Give advance warning of briefs in the pipeline especially ones with tight deadlines. What do they find gets great work from their department? Show interest and respect for them and their craft. Appreciate their expertise and experience in their specific subject.

Be flexible. Be prepared to re-allocate priorities and deadlines, where possible, on different projects. Give options and choice. Be seen to fight their case with clients and be seen to have argued for more time for their contribution. Keep it interesting and challenging for them. Ensure they experience a sense of growth and personal achievement. Give detailed feedback – as objectively as possible. Push the client for this too ('The client didn't like it' is not feedback).

• **Create a sense of 'we'**

Make sure they feel fully involved in the development and success of the client's business. It should be a collaborative effort. Be enthusiastic about the brief and the work. If you aren't excited then how can you expect them to be? Your enthusiasm and passion will be contagious. Argue their case; don't be seen as weak when selling risky work. This will encourage them to produce more interesting work next time. Ensure they have access and face-time with the client so they take ownership of the relationship and a sense of responsibility. Develop a problem-solving attitude together.

• **Understand their self-interest**

See how they benefit. People do things for their reasons, not yours.

They may be motivated in different ways to you. Find out what their big picture is and what their goals are. WIIFM: What's in it for me? Put yourself in their shoes. See it from their perspective. What do they value?

- **Give praise and recognition**

Praise and recognition are such powerful motivators. Make sure they get credit for their contribution in front of the client, senior agency management and their boss. Thank them for their work, especially great work. The thanks need to be genuine, timely and specific. Have a sense of fun with your thanks. Take time to celebrate great work and hard work.

- **Build a healthy respectful business relationship**

You are in it for the long term. You want to win the war not the battle. Choose carefully which battles to fight. Take time to earn your colleagues' respect. You don't get respect through your title; you get it through your deeds. Walk your Talk. Be genuine and authentic. Use humour and a light touch.

Be assertive where necessary. Choose your language and demeanour carefully. Have high standards for yourself and for them. Hold them accountable for their work and you with yours. Show humility, as a last resort! Be prepared to apologise on those very rare occasions when you might get something wrong!

- **When there are problems with the client**

Be seen by your colleagues to resolve and improve any problem situations with the client. Be honest about what you can change and what you can't. Explain to your client the importance of great teamwork and how they can help you to help them to produce great work. Praise from clients directly to your colleagues will also be valuable.

Negotiating with suppliers

Do you negotiate effectively with your suppliers?

When you negotiate effectively with your suppliers as well as with your clients, you are now moving towards an even more profitable business model.

Put yourself in the supplier's shoes; what would be important to you? What would you value? As a supplier/provider yourself, you should have sufficient empathy to understand their situation. Much of what has been written about negotiations with clients in previous chapters will apply to negotiating with suppliers: the need for rigorous preparation; understanding your bottom line; being clear about your ideal, target and walk-away; anticipating responses; your assertiveness and so on. So we won't repeat those. I will focus on four key points:

1. Win-win. Mutual satisfaction.

2. The extra profitability derived from negotiating effectively with suppliers.

3. Your supplier wish list.

4. Questions to ask suppliers.

1. Win-win. Mutual satisfaction.

If the supplier is an ongoing provider of services to your business, and you plan to keep it that way, I recommend you seek a win-win relationship that is based on long-term trust and enables both parties to prosper. Otherwise, playing the tough negotiator with your trusted suppliers may get you some short-term benefits, but long-term there is a danger they won't be there to support you when you most need them.

Look after your suppliers and they will be more willing to support you if you go through a difficult period.

Always pass on supplier conditions to your clients such as deadlines, extras, payment terms, briefing requirements, specifications and delivery details.

Never commit an order to a supplier without the client having committed the order to your agency first and in writing.

You may be surprised that I need to write this and emphasise it so strongly. A senior and very experienced manager at an agency placed orders with suppliers without client approval. The client did not proceed with the job and the agency was around £100,000 out of pocket.

Some years ago, British Airways negotiated very hard with Gate Gourmet who provided the airline with in-flight meals. BA drove Gate

Gourmet's price so low it resulted in the wages being paid to Gate Gourmet's staff also being very low – so low in fact that Gate Gourmet's staff went on strike demanding more money. The strike caused BA huge problems in the supply of their in-flight meals and a huge PR embarrassment for several months. Is the fault solely with BA? Of course not; Gate Gourmet must take responsibility for quoting such low prices to BA and having a business model based on 'below minimum wages.' Yes, negotiate hard with suppliers but not so hard that you shoot yourself in the foot. BA must also take some responsibility for seeking such a Win-Lose negotiation.

It is often unclear what value is to an organisation until things go wrong. BA was probably unaware of the effects of their relationship breakdown with Gate Gourmet until it was too late.

If the supplier is a one-off provider, are the gloves off? I'd say 'no.' Treat them with respect but negotiate hard. Your prime concern in a one-off negotiation is for you to WIN.

2. The extra profitability derived from negotiating effectively with suppliers.

In the chapter on Pricing we looked at the danger of discounting fees and prices to clients and the corresponding impact on profitability.

Price you sell at	£10	£9 (10 % reduction)
Cost to buy	£8	£8
Your gross margin	£2	£1
Units	100	200 (twice as many for the same profit)
Gross profit	£200	£200

So how does this work if we also negotiate more effectively with suppliers? Imagine if we can buy 10 % better from our supplier. This means our gross margin increases by 40% and simply selling the same number of units means a 40% increase in gross profit.

Price you sell at	£10	£10
Cost to buy	£8	£7.20 (10% improvement in buying price)
Your gross margin	£2	£2.80
Units	100	100
Gross profit	£200	£280 (40% improvement in gross profit)

If this is coupled with other financial concessions such as preferential payment terms, it can make a significant impact on your bottom line.

Always provide written confirmation of your order or a Purchase Order (when you are busy and under pressure it is easy to forget this).

3. Your supplier wish list.

With clients, we considered the benefit of a wish list of tradable items. The same approach can be taken with suppliers. Develop a list of tradables that are valuable to you with your suppliers such as:

- Introductory discounts
- Volume discounts
- Delivery included
- Payment terms

4. Questions to ask suppliers.

Preparing your questions to ask suppliers can help to put you in a powerful front-foot mindset. The reaction to your preparation and questions from the supplier will tell you a considerable amount about their need to do business, to sell to you and their negotiation experience. There is a need for you to behave in an ethical way when negotiating with suppliers, otherwise you become the monster client from hell.

Some interesting questions to ask suppliers:

- What's special about your company?

- Why should we do business with you?

- Can I talk to some of your other recent satisfied customers?

- Tell me, what would be valuable to you if we were to work together?

- We've had a number of quotes from similar suppliers, how can you improve yours further?

- We want to work with you but have a substantially cheaper quote from another company – would you reconsider your price?

Supplier review

If you want to take a more strategic approach to your supplier management, then set up a Supplier Review. This should be an annual process.

Identify your top suppliers from the past 12 months (10 companies?). Analyse your spend with them over the past three to five years to show scale and growth of business. Identify where the majority of your money to suppliers is going. This is likely to be an area of potential saving. Assess your likely supplier requirements going forward. How is your business changing and that of your clients? More of the same, or changing requirements, or changing scale of purchase?

Do your homework on each key supplier. Gather subjective feedback from colleagues on each supplier's performance and ability/attitude to resolving any problems arising. Review their and your Terms & Conditions. Optional information: review your top 10 suppliers' accounts via Companies House or Dunn & Bradstreet to see how important your business is to their overall sales, what percentage of their business does your business account for and when is their financial year end. This gives you an indication as to areas of possible flexibility and leverage. Meet with suppliers individually on an annual basis.

Do any existing suppliers seem complacent, not leading-edge or tired? Look at alternative providers. Review the marketplace for other new suppliers to ensure you have a suitable roster of suppliers. Benchmark some prices to check their pricing. Don't just seek the lowest price; look for the best value, their expertise and quality of work.

Plan your strategy with each top 10 supplier. Retain, place more business or replace etc. Negotiate improved deals. Log and collate all the improved deals and agreements achieved. Consider how this could be improved in the following year.

Communicate internally and ensure colleagues are aware of any changes agreed with suppliers. Advise colleagues of any preferred suppliers and new agreements.

'But I find it hard negotiating with suppliers I've known for several years. I feel awkward.'

It is common for agency account handlers to say this to me. My response is always the same:

'Your first responsibility is to your company, then to your clients and then to your suppliers. You are a professional and this is a business, not a social club. You need to be assertive and tougher. Part of your employment responsibility is to manage suppliers and their service for the benefit of your clients. Use some of your 'buyer' leverage in the same way clients do with you. You can still negotiate firmly and fairly with suppliers whilst maintaining a good professional and business-like relationship with them.'

In the past five years, Procurement has increased its involvement with agencies. Some agencies find this very challenging and others have found it has improved the client-agency process. This is the subject of the next chapter.

CHAPTER 10

Procurement

Key learnings

- Procurement, their increasing importance and their perspective

- Anticipating their approach

- How to work better with them

How much do you lose each year because you are not equipped to negotiate with Procurement?

This chapter is towards the end of the book because it is likely you will require the full breadth of your negotiation skills to negotiate with your client's Procurement team. Procurement has become far more powerful and influential. It cannot be ignored or avoided.

So who are Procurement? They are a dedicated team of specialist purchasing professionals. Their sole purpose is to procure, on behalf of their company, all or most of their company's purchases. They will be looking to reduce costs and save money while reducing their company's exposure to risk. Some see themselves as 'financial guardians' for their company, ensuring best practice in all aspects of buying.

Procurement specialists are found mainly within larger corporate companies and government departments. Their primary focus is on the major areas of spend as these are seen as having the most potential for improvement and savings.

Is it simply a case of *'Show me the money'* from the film Jerry McGuire?

> *Sometimes what counts can't be counted*
> *and what can be counted doesn't count.*
> Albert Einstein

As well as looking to reduce cost, they will also be aiming to reduce or remove subjectivity in the decision-making process. They will want their company and marketing colleagues to appoint, and then work with, an agency appointed for predominantly objective reasons. They can see the close 'relationship' between the marketing client and agency as potentially clouding the judgement of their marketing colleagues.

Campaign magazine had a wonderful quote a few years ago about Procurement:

> *They poke and prod where the sun don't shine.*

As the level of money spent by clients with agencies has increased, so has the level of involvement by Procurement. The cost savings provided by Procurement have been huge. Methods have included benchmarking, e-auctions, fee consultants and periodic pitches.

Businesses are opportunistic and must often make harsh business decisions. You may find that when you deal with Procurement you have to make some harsh and difficult business decisions. Remember that the ultimate choice is always yours.

How has Procurement affected agencies? Has Procurement's involvement been a benefit or a disadvantage to agencies?

Procurement has certainly affected many agencies – some in a good way and some in not such a good way. Different agencies have shared experiences with me about their interactions with their clients' Procurement departments that have appalled me. The behaviour of the Procurement specialist sometimes verges on bullying and threatening; in a nutshell, unprofessional. I have also been told by agencies of having pitched for a project for ongoing work to then be told they now need to enter an e-auction.

In other cases, agencies have found the involvement of Procurement has improved the processes, quality of briefs and methods of working with their client.

In other cases, the Procurement specialist has benchmarked the prices of a range of agency services compared to other agencies; they have then instructed the agency to match the lowest price. In some of the worst cases, the behaviour by Procurement has included threats such as, 'If you don't drop your fees by xx% you will never work with ABC company again,' and, 'Drop your fees or we will put the business out to pitch.'

In fairness to those Procurement specialists, benchmarking is a vital part of their job and is a very sensible process. The agency has free choice as to whether to drop their price. In addition, the agency should be working hard to differentiate itself from its agency competitors so that a decision to work with one agency compared to another is not based solely on their prices. The agency should be developing a range of differentiated selling propositions to counter-balance differences in price. These differentiated selling propositions could include:

- Specific expertise

- Specific experience

- Techniques or processes

- Contacts

- Creativity

- Results

- Awards

- People

- Network of offices

- Or a combination of the above

I recently met a Procurement director working in a major corporate company and I asked him how he tackled negotiations with suppliers in general.

"It's very simple. I'm clear beforehand about what I want. I go into the meeting and demand what I want. I give nothing. I don't come out of the meeting till I've got what I want."

I then asked, "So do you always get what you want?" He smiled and said, "Oh, yes!"

When you are negotiating with someone with that much clarity and determination, you had better be well prepared and have decided what your options are, your concessions and your walk-away point.

Supplier delusion

Procurement specialists have a wonderful term, 'Supplier delusion.' This is when the agency or supplier may believe they are in a partnership arrangement with a customer; however, the client buying organisation has a very different picture. There may be situations where the agency invests time, money and effort relentlessly into the relationship; however, the client will always keep the agency at arm's length.

Do client's Procurement departments lie?

An agency related to me their recent Procurement experience with their client, a major international corporate. The client employed a range of different agencies. To the advertising agency they had demanded 'a 40% reduction in fees with no change to the account team.' The agency agreed a substantial reduction – around 25%. The client then went to the digital agency and demanded 'a 40% reduction in fees with no change to the account team.' The digital agency was told that the ad agency had agreed to the 40% reduction (a lie). The digital agency agreed to a 15% reduction in fee.

The client then went to the PR agency and demanded 'a 40% reduction in fees with no change to the account team.' The PR agency was told that the ad agency and the digital agency had both agreed to the 40% reduction (double lie). The PR agency agreed a 25% reduction in fee. Each agency had been played off against the other.

Independent Procurement specialists seem to be the most ruthless. Typically, they are independent of the client company and are rewarded partly or wholly based on the savings they achieve. Some claim to have agency experience and say that they know just how to 'winkle-out overspend' and achieve huge cost savings. Some claim to have benchmark prices for a range of agency services.

These independent Procurement specialists have no vested interest in whether the client-agency relationship subsequently works or not. Their priority is simply to make cuts and savings. Often they are simply rewarded based on the savings they make for the client.

I have attended Procurement conferences and seminars and read their trade publications in order to better understand Procurement's perspective, their attitudes and their thinking. While attending one Procurement conference in 2009 during the height of the recession (or should that be the low of the recession?), one speaker asked the audience of over 100 Procurement specialists, "Who sees the recession as a great opportunity for Procurement?" Well over 95 % agreed that the recession was a great opportunity for Procurement. They were then able to explain why they saw it as an opportunity. Some of the reasons given were:

- "We can put even more pressure on the prices from our suppliers because many are desperate."

- "We can tear up contracts and re-negotiate prices while their business is down."

- "My CEO thinks my Procurement department is brilliant as we've given him a £2m saving, unlike my colleague the marketing director..."

- "We've demanded a 10 % reduction in the day-rate paid to all our contractors and freelance staff. We gave them 24 hours notice to decide. They nearly all agreed."

Unprofitable clients rarely have a happy team. If you treat an agency as a supplier, you will eventually get a commodity.
Martin Sorrell

Put yourself in the shoes of your client's Procurement person

Would you be so different? So how do they see their role and agencies? Some of them believe that agencies are making too much money from their clients. (This was further exacerbated by an ISBA report in 2010 in which many clients still believe that agencies are making too much money. Given that perception is more important than reality, then if that's what many clients believe, then it is hardly surprising that Procurement people feel the same).

Procurement sees expenditure with suppliers that has not been agreed and approved centrally on their approved supplier list as 'maverick expenditure' or 'grey expenditure.' Many senior Procurement people are targeting to get this down to below 5% of their overall company spend. In some major corporates, to ensure this is taken seriously by those who commit the 'crime' of spending maverick expenditure, they receive a warning letter, firstly from the Finance Director. If the 'crime' is repeated they then receive a warning letter from the CEO.

Procurement sees the world of business differently to agency people. They often see themselves as a profit centre. They will use a variety of aggresive negotiation techniques to pressurise agencies. They won't accept an agency's first price and will push for continuous improvement in prices and efficiencies. They will avoid letting an agency know they are under time pressure and will be wary of agencies exploiting their position. They will deliberately be unpredictable and know too well the power of pauses and silence. They will want to know how important and attractive the client company is to the agency and may even put a valuation on having their name on the agency's client list or website, whilst at the same time they will be concerned about being too important for the agency and whether the agency has sufficient capacity.

Procurement people are also interested in what they call 'total cost of ownership.' They want to understand the longer-term financial implications for their company. As you can see, Procurement can have a huge influence on the ultimate performance and profitability of their company and your agency.

So what have Procurement done for agencies? The best professional Procurement specialists recognise the importance of factors over and above simply price. In some cases they have improved the briefing process for agencies, ensuring the agency receives a well thought through and written brief. Procurement best practice has ensured that the agency receives a Purchase Order before starting work and committing expenditure. In some cases they have improved the pitch process, ensuring fairness and clarity for those participating. Some have streamlined agency rosters so there is a healthy level of work for those on the roster rather than many agencies scrabbling around for crumbs.

The best Procurement specialists recognise that the best client-agency relationships are based on win-win and on shared objectives; that it's not just about the cheapest price but about value for money, value for time etc. That a positive, constructive working relationship based on trust achieves far more than one based on fear and aggression. The best Procurement specialists have worked hard to develop their understanding of marketing, marketing services, agencies and the creative output. Quality is important to them but at the same time it must be fit for purpose. They understand that sharing knowledge enables the agency to develop winning solutions far more readily than keeping the agency at arm's length. They see Procurement best practice as good business practice. They believe that by being demanding, Procurement can achieve a high-quality agency service.

Magic and Logic

The IPA (Institute of Practitioners in Advertising), CIPS (The Chartered Institute of Purchasing and Supply) and ISBA (Incorporated Society of British Advertisers) developed an approach to the 'client-Procurement-agency' relationship triangle. They developed the approach 'Magic and Logic.' This was to separate two key agency tasks and suggested a different method of charging for the Magic versus the Logic – the Magic being the inspired thinking and creative idea generation, the Logic being the implementation and delivery of the idea and campaign management. This was a useful step in improving the understanding of each party and I look forward to seeing this develop further.

For agencies, I think it is time to stop moaning about Procurement. Learn to live and work with them. They are here to stay. See what you can do to improve your negotiation position.

- Sharpen up your negotiation skills among the senior agency team particularly. Ideally do this for the whole team.

- Differentiate your agency in ways that clients value and are prepared to pay more for. Get real clarity as to the value clients derive from you. What are they prepared to pay good money for and what do they see as a commodity? Move up the 'food-chain' to deal with more senior decision-makers, not the budget gate-keepers.

- Look for ways to improve the efficiency of your business whilst maintaining or improving the quality of service clients receive.

- Update your business to be in tune with changing media choices, changing markets, changing customers, changing technology and a globalised world. (Your competitors are no longer on your doorstep; increasingly they are, and will be, from countries such as India, China, Brazil and Eastern Europe).

- Ensure your business is well spread across a range of clients and in different industry sectors.

- Get real clarity as to the value clients derive from you. What are they prepared to pay good money for and what is a commodity? Move up the 'food-chain' to deal with more senior decision-makers, not the budget gate-keepers.

- Raise your game, personally. Develop your expertise and critical business thinking. Be the best you can be.

- Some believe that the rules of the game have changed and maybe even the game has changed. Agencies need to play differently with new skills.

Meeting with Procurement

So you have a meeting with your key client's Procurement Director to discuss fees and rates for the coming year. It's in two weeks time; what do you do, besides panic?

Over the previous six months, I would hope that you will have been developing your understanding of your value to your client. After each project and campaign you have evaluated the results and benefit to the client. You've compared the results with the original brief and objectives. You have quantified and monetised your value to your client. You've sought quotes and testimonials from your key marketing client contacts to endorse your work and value.

You've ensured the client is providing quality written briefs, minimised scope creep, pushed back on unreasonable deadlines and unnecessary changes to projects. You've ensured a healthy spread of business across the agency, pursuing profitable work and categorised clients and their work into 'profit vampires,' 'middle of the road' and 'lucrative'. You've been selective over which new business opportunities to pursue and invest your time in. So hopefully you are in good shape.

In advance of the meeting with Procurement you need to prepare diligently. See Procurement as an opportunity but be prepared for all eventualities. Be clear what you want from the deal. Decide your priorities.

In advance of the meeting, phone the senior Procurement person, introduce yourself and explain how you are looking forward to meeting them. Most agencies won't do this. Ask what exactly they would like to get from the meeting and what their priorities are. What do they want you to do in advance of the meeting? Most agencies won't do this. This suggests a level of confidence and a professional business approach. Their answer to what they want from the meeting and their language will tell you a lot about their priorities and enable you to plan with your eyes wide open (rather than burying your head in the sand dreading the meeting). Is their focus on 'cost, cost, cost' or do they see the bigger picture of 'cost, value, quality and results'?

Do your research. Google them and do a LinkedIn search. Phone your marketing client(s). What is their perspective on the meeting? What advice can they provide? How well have Procurement meetings with the other agencies gone? Can Marketing be present at the meeting? Phone the other agencies, assuming you have good relationships, to understand their experience of meeting with Procurement.

You can then plan and prepare for the meeting. Decide who should attend. I'd recommend your Finance Director and the director heading up the business. Prepare hard measures and results to show your value and contribution. Show the return on investment that their company's marketing spend with your agency has generated. Show how you have achieved given sales targets and other tangible quantitative measures. Show the projections going forward. Position their spend with you as 'investment' not as 'costs.' Think through the downside: what would be the cost to the client company of not running this activity?

Clarify and craft how your agency provides a differentiated service matching the specific requirement of the client. Don't be satisfied with generic truisms they can hear from other agencies. (Value, like beauty, is in the eye of the beholder). Don't assume. Be able to articulate benefits that will resonate with the client company and Procurement. Put yourself in their shoes. What would 'you' want from 'you'? What would you ask for or demand from 'you'?

Anticipate the tough questions and challenges you are likely to receive from Procurement. Then brainstorm and plan your potential answers. Think through how you will handle their questions:

Examples of challenging questions from Procurement can include:

- What are your costs of running the business?

- How much profit are you making from our business?

- What rebates do you get from suppliers?

- What are the salaries of the team?

- What efficiency improvements have you made which you can pass on to us?

- How will your recommendations be measured and what are your methods for doing this?

Decide in advance what areas of questions are taboo for you to answer and are not up for discussion. Some Procurement people ask to know the complete overhead breakdown for the agency and the salary packages of the individuals working on their account. I believe this is personal information and a breach of employee confidentiality. I believe this information is irrelevant to them and actually none of their business. Perhaps you can provide them with guidelines or salary bands and a multiplier to show the broad team cost to include an overhead allocation.

Beware of showing they are your most important client. Explain that they are in your top three or five. This avoids them feeling they have got the upper hand. Avoid telling them how much of your business they account for or provide the lowest credible figure.

Plan your perceptive questions to ask them. What are their criteria for evaluating..? Over and above price, what else is important to the business? What is the order of priority of importance of these factors?

If you want to reduce the price, then what do you want to take out?

Understand the level of profitability that this client accounts for to your agency. How has this changed over the past three years? On current projections how is it likely to change going forward?

Identify potential ways to improve the processes and ways of working. Are there any easy cost-savings? What's your ideal, target, walk-away? What are your must-haves, like-to-haves and non-negotiables? What's your BATNA? Consider some different options for how the account can be run at different pricing/fee levels. Consider what concessions you would consider trading in exchange for any financial reductions.

Consider how a 'risk/reward' remuneration could work for both parties. Keep the measures simple and transparent. Make sure this is all carefully documented and signed off by senior management in each company (agency and client). There have been a few cases of client companies reneging on the PBR reward payout to their agency. Tread carefully.

How will you be in the right state for the meeting? How will you ensure your level of confidence and self-belief is just right, not over-confident but 'a little south of arrogant?' Where is the meeting and how will you ensure you arrive early or on time? Ensure you are highly organised with your files, documentation and paperwork. (Some Procurement people seem to have OCD, Obsessive Compulsive Disorder).

Consider running a rehearsal for the meeting. Be prepared to walk away. Be prepared to say 'no.'

No client should be so important to you that you cannot walk away.

• At the meeting

Approach the meeting with an open and friendly attitude, but be ready for conflict. Be well organised and arrive early. Have your files and documentation well organised. Find ways to demonstrate your professionalism. Ensure you have an air of confidence and that your body language doesn't give away any tell-tale signs. You need to be in the right mindset.

Make sure you and your colleague(s) are 'on the same page' and have agreed roles. The agency Finance Director can take a much firmer role and play the bad cop. If your marketing client(s) are there, beware of being seen as having too close a relationship. Procurement may see the relationship as compromising the decision-making ability of your marketing client.

Don't just talk about price all the time. Talk more about the business, results and future deliverables. (Some Procurement people have told me how sales people can be obsessed with talking about money which then encourages the Procurement person to oblige and also talk about money!) Be prepared to think creatively about possible solutions and ways of working. Do not agree to anything that was not pre-agreed back at the agency or anything you feel uncertain about. If necessary, give yourself time to think.

- 'This is a big request. I will have to discuss this with my board/finance team/senior management.'

- 'This will be a problem. I will need to review the numbers again and come back to you tomorrow.'

If you do give Procurement any fee reductions or major concessions, take time to think through the implications for your relationship with your marketing client. (There is a danger of making your marketing client look like they have been a soft option for the past few years).

An agency was telling me how they reduced their annual fee by over £150,000 in an e-auction. The agency was the incumbent. Dropping the fee by such a large amount puts the marketing client in a difficult position. It looks like the marketing client was incompetent and was paying far too much for the past three years.

Make sure you agree that 'these revised terms are to stand for a minimum of one/two/three years.' (Some Procurement people make a habit of coming back six months later looking for more reduction and concessions).

If Procurement do become aggressive, stay calm. Decide what level of assertiveness you need to use. The more generous you are to the other party and the quicker you give in to them, the more they will want. Procurement will see your generosity as weakness and simply ask for more, either now or in the near future. Remind the client of the monetised value they have received. Before you give a concession, get a concession.

If you give in to bullies, the relationship will always be abusive and out of balance. Although it is really tough to do so, you must have a clear, pre-agreed walk-away position. If they do use threatening behaviour then simply ask open questions without showing you are on the defensive. You cannot turn a really tough hard-nosed negotiator into a collaborative problem-solving partner. If all else fails:

Give them what they want, but on your terms.

At the end of the meeting, summarise your understanding of the key principles agreed and any actions on either side. Document the key points.

• Back at the office

Document and log your learnings from the meeting. What did you do right? What did you do wrong? What would you do differently? What would you do next time to improve? Share your findings with other colleagues likely to be having similar meetings with their client's Procurement department. Keep this learning log close at hand because the next meeting with another client's Procurement department won't be too far away.

So how do we put all this into practice? How do we develop the right habits? How do we reap the rewards of our negotiation skills, self-belief and front-foot mindset?

If you know but do not do, you do not know.

Negotiation is a mindset and is like a muscle. It needs to be used regularly. Use it or lose it. The next chapter looks at how we can develop our negotiation momentum.

CHAPTER 11

In conclusion

How will you ensure that both parties feel highly satisfied?

Negotiating more effectively with your clients and prospects can have a huge impact on your agency and you individually. I consistently receive feedback from my clients that they feel more confident, more able to construct improved deals and enjoy improved profitability. When this happens, the client generally also experiences an improvement in satisfaction too. A real win-win.

This won't happen automatically. The negotiation mindset needs to become second nature for your people. The agency needs to develop the right agency culture to achieve great negotiations, improved profitability and achieve success. Your people need to feel confident to apply their negotiation skills.

Develop a real understanding across the agency of the importance of value, quality work, client results, fair remuneration, great relationships and what profitability is. Tighten up your scope of work with clients to include what's in scope and what's out of scope and set up SLAs – Service Level Agreements.

Be selective about choosing which clients are right for the agency. Pick those for whom you can produce great work and who understand fair remuneration and an appropriate long-term trusted adviser relationship. Ensure you are far enough up the 'food-chain' and working directly with the C-Suite and decision-makers. Ensure a good spread of clients – ideally no client bigger than 15 % of the business.

There is a difficult trade-off between specialising in one or two areas and also having a healthy spread of clients. Develop your niches and expertise. However, beware of too many clients in one sector, e.g. government, travel, financial services, otherwise the agency can be disproportionately affected by macro-economic changes such as 9/11, a financial crisis and major cuts in government spending or government policy changes.

Have quarterly reviews with the client, at senior level, assessing the value created and the results achieved. Ask the client to articulate the agency's contribution to their business. Provide two-way feedback to improve the quality of briefs, the quality of response, thinking and creative output. Ask for referrals to other like-minded senior client contacts.

Be selective about choosing the right people for your agency. Choose bright, confident and assertive people who understand the value they can produce and have a problem-solving attitude. Choose those who can think creatively, independently and critically, not just people who are simply able to deliver and implement.

Make negotiations and profitability a core KPI (Key Performance Indicator) for the agency and senior individuals at the agency. Have negotiation as a key topic on each monthly management meeting/

board meeting agenda. Review negotiations over the previous month, successes achieved, disappointments experienced and lessons learnt. Share what worked and what didn't. Keep a log of negotiated extra money and concessions. Then discuss upcoming client negotiations and how best to prepare and handle those negotiations effectively.

Tackle problems between the agency and client early while they are still small and before they grow and you reach the point of no return.

Encourage your people to learn to negotiate more effectively with their clients and to appreciate that negotiation is a life-skill which will have important implications for them.

Plan changes to the teams on each client account in terms of the individuals. Perhaps change one or two people a year on each key account; this injects freshness, allows subtle changes to the overhead base on each account and manages client's expectations for change on the team.

Avoid people working 100 % on any one client. Working on more than one client keeps the individuals fresher and stretched whilst allowing the optimisation of resource allocation.

One of the most common reasons given at exit interviews by people leaving agencies is, 'I feel bored, I feel unchallenged, I'm not growing. I want fresh challenges.' If you want to keep your best people, stretch them and keep them challenged with fresh opportunities to give them a real sense of achievement and personal growth. Give them the negotiation skills so they can achieve their potential.

Track agency profitability by client and reward profitability improvement through better negotiations, not just working harder. For example, an increased annual fee, reducing scope creep and improving the client-agency relationship balance.

Develop strategies and actions for the three types of client: profit vampires, middle of the road and lucratives.

Review your supplier base. Conduct an annual supplier review. View ongoing core suppliers as critical relationships.

And for you personally....

Negotiating is like a muscle that needs to be used on a regular basis to keep it toned and at peak level. It requires regular practice to maintain your confidence level. It is also necessary to be constantly alert and on the look-out for opportunities to negotiate effectively with clients, prospects and suppliers. So how can you develop this skill as second nature?

- **Have fun and enjoy developing your ability:** enjoy finding new questions to ask, new ways to handle tough questions and objections and enjoy using the key negotiation strategies and principles.

- **Outside of work:** practise using your negotiation ability in your personal life in shops, hotels, with tradespeople and best of all with your children.

- **Continuous learning:** like any skill, develop yourself through continuous learning by attending seminars, researching and reading.

Lightning Source UK Ltd.
Milton Keynes UK
UKOW022139221211

184281UK00001B/22/P